Welcome

Welcome to the Kent Mu
The museum was purpo
1933. It has always been open to the general public.

The museum is set out in a way that anyone who is not a Freemason can learn something of what it is, the history and how it operates today. It was redesigned in 2012 to better explain the objectives of Freemasonry.

This guide will help during your tour of the museum as it follows the different sections. It also adds some further information. We hope you enjoy your visit.

The oak double doors as you enter the museum were obtained from a large house in Hales Place, Canterbury. The house had been used for a variety of purposes, the last as a Jesuit college. It was demolished but the doors were saved for the museum.

The inner glass doors, together with the stained glass windows, came from the old Grand Lodge in Great Queen Street, London.

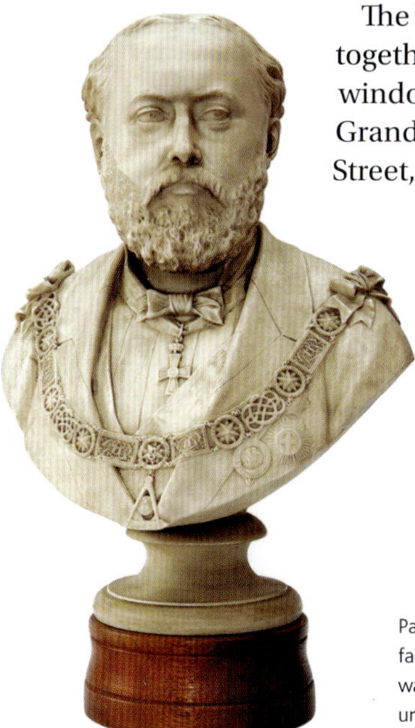

Parian bust by the Copeland factory of **King Edward VII**. He was Grand Master from 1875 until he became king in 1901.

Part of the window with **the coat of arms of King Edward VII**.

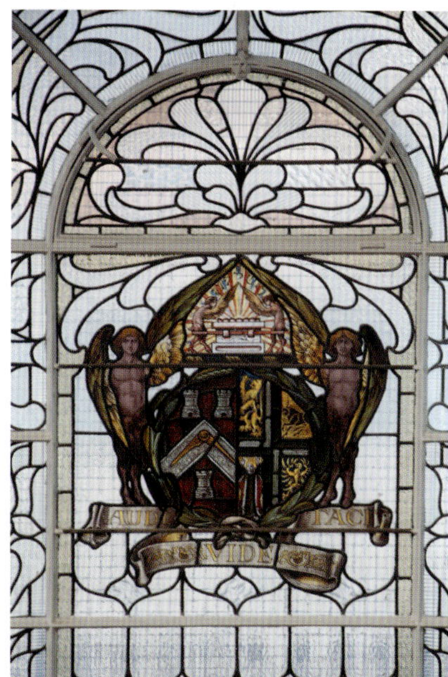

What is Freemasonry?

In simple terms, Freemasonry is a system of morality, which, as we masons say, is 'a progressive science veiled in allegory and illustrated by symbols.' It is not a religion, although to be a member you have to have a belief in a Supreme Being. The first question put to a potential candidate is 'Do you believe in God?' If the answer is No, then he is not eligible to join. If it is Yes, then it does not matter if he is a Christian, Jew, Moslem, Sikh, Hindu, Buddhist, or follows any other formal religion or follows his own way, he may be admitted. The other qualification is that he is over 21 years (usually) and is of good character. The aim is to take good men and make them better people.

The new mason must go through three ceremonies, called the First, Second and Third Degrees. At the third, he becomes a fully-fledged Master Mason. Each Degree requires an obligation to be taken each time on the Volume of the Sacred Law, usually the Holy Bible but it may be the appropriate holy book for his religion.

King James Bible of 1613 with masonic symbols on the cover.

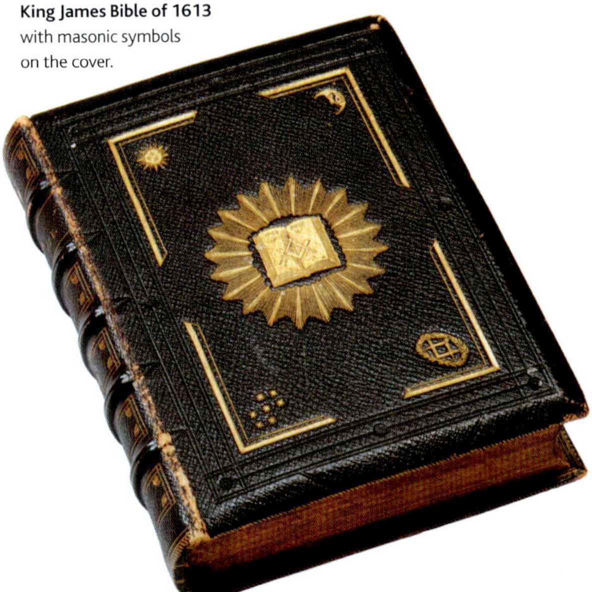

After taking the Third Degree, the mason receives his **Grand Lodge certificate**. The certificate here is in English and Latin. Today they are in English only.

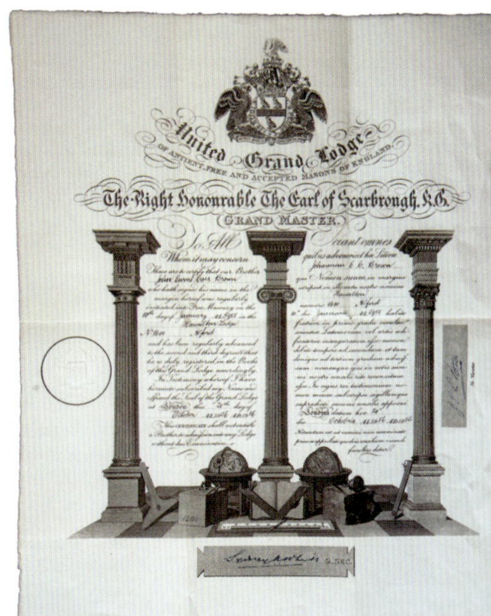

Famous and Not-so-famous Freemasons

On display in the museum are photographs of some famous and local Freemasons. This is intended to show how widespread Freemasonry extends across society, including among its members royalty, clergymen, film stars and musicians.

Famous Freemasons:

George Washington, first President of the United States

'Jack' Dempsey, boxer

Billy Butlin, holiday camp entrepreneur

Sir Winston Churchill, Prime Minister

Sir Ernest Shackleton, explorer

Robert Burns, poet

Harry Houdini, escapologist

Sir Len Hutton, cricketer

Sir Alf Ramsey, footballer and manager

The Duke of Wellington, soldier and Prime Minister

Sir Arthur Conan Doyle, author

King George VI

Buzz Aldrin, astronaut

John Wayne, actor

Sir Alexander Fleming, scientist

Buffalo Bill, Wild West showman

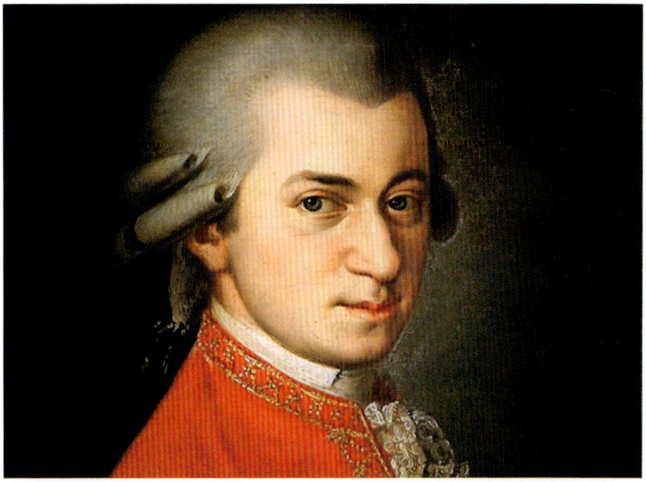

Wolfgang Amadeus Mozart, composer. His operas have masonic influences.

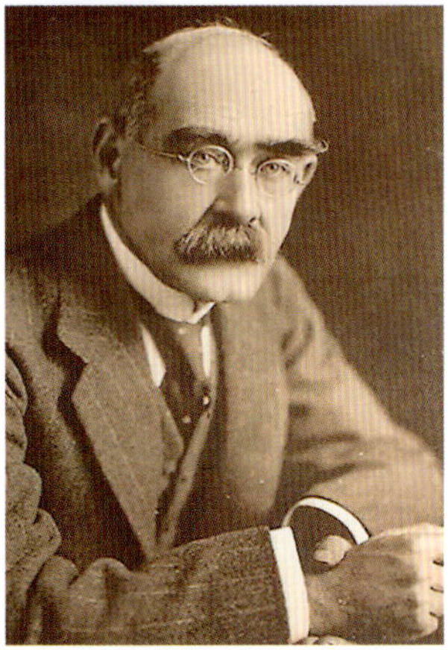

Rudyard Kipling, author. He brings Freemasonry into his books, including *The Man Who Would Be King* (1888).

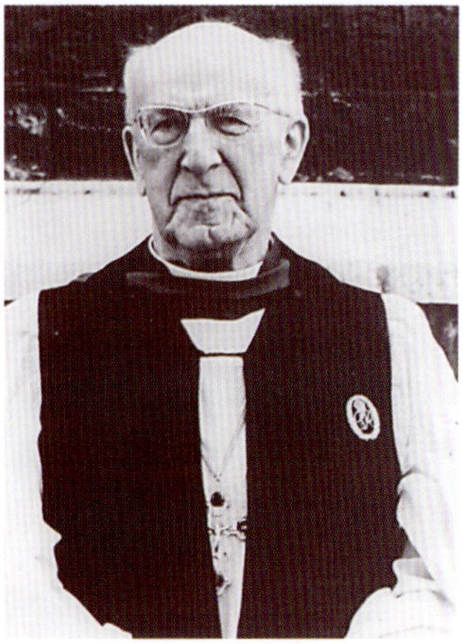

Geoffrey Fisher, archbishop. He was Archbishop of Canterbury at the time of the Queen's coronation. He can be seen in pictures placing the crown on her head.

Origins of Freemasonry

The precise origin of Freemasonry is obscure. Lodges of operative masons (practising stonemasons) existed in mediaeval England and built famous cathedrals, abbeys and castles, including Canterbury Cathedral. Operative masons developed guilds and lodges to regulate their 'craft', and they were divided into apprentices, craftsmen and masters, terms still used to describe the Three Degrees of Masonry today.

Operative masons used various signs and passwords to identify each other. They also marked their work, so that the stonework they had prepared could be identified. You can still see some of their marks on the stones of Canterbury Cathedral.

By the seventeenth century the wealthy and educated in society had adapted the organisation of the operatives into the lodges we have today. Instead of *using* the working tools, they gave each a moral significance. The square suggests you treat fellow man 'squarely', and a 24-inch gauge teaches us the 24 hours of the day should be spent in work, refreshment, prayer and service to others. Hence Freemasons are known as 'speculative' as opposed to 'operative' masons.

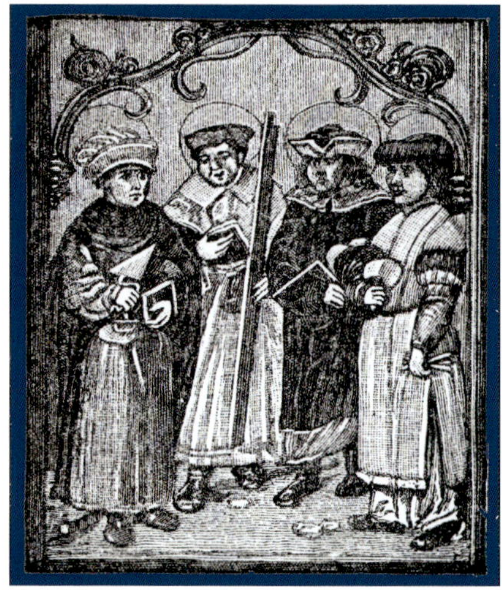

ABOVE: **Mediaeval operative masons** and their working tools.

BELOW: **The Freemasons' working tools** as ivory miniatures. Left to right: a 24-inch gauge, compasses (top), level (below), plumb rule, square, gavel and trowel.

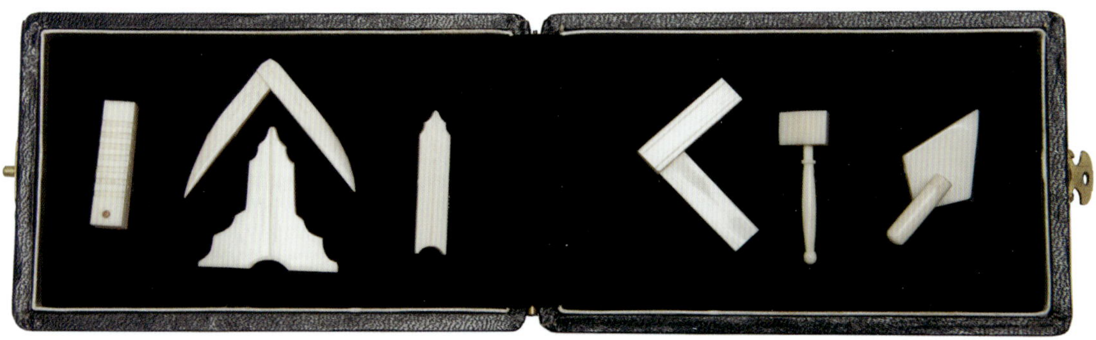

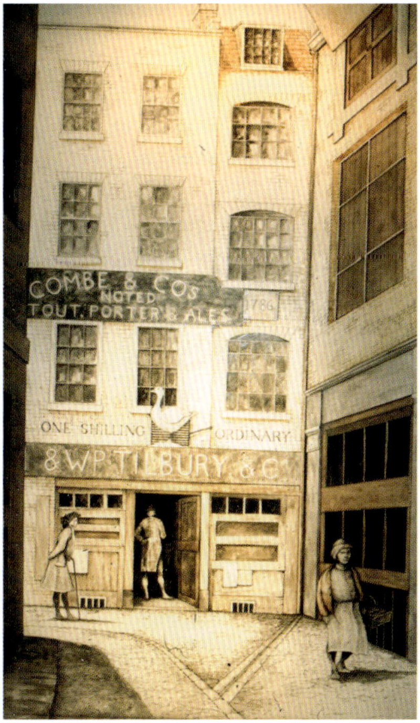

LEFT: **The Goose and Gridiron**.

In 1717 four lodges met together at the Goose and Gridiron alehouse in St Paul's Churchyard, London, and formed the first Grand Lodge, appointing the first Grand Master.

From this small beginning, modern Freemasonry spread to Europe, the Americas and beyond. Today the United Grand Lodge of England has almost 8,000 lodges, meeting in England, Wales and overseas. Scotland and Ireland have their own Grand Lodges, as do many countries of the world.

BELOW: Two eighteenth-century **masonic aprons**.

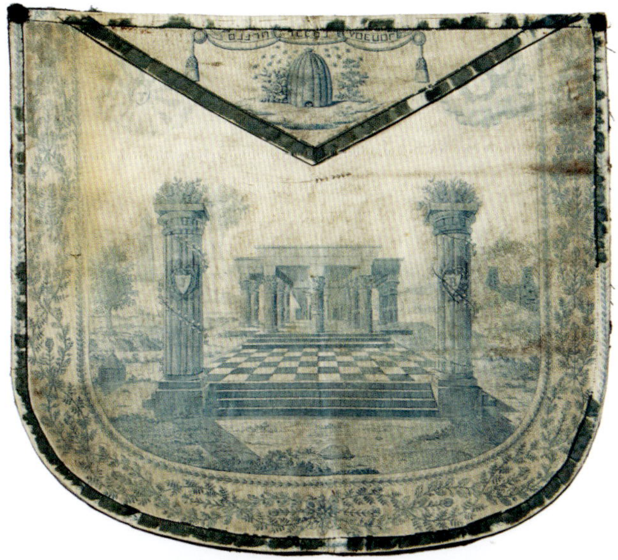

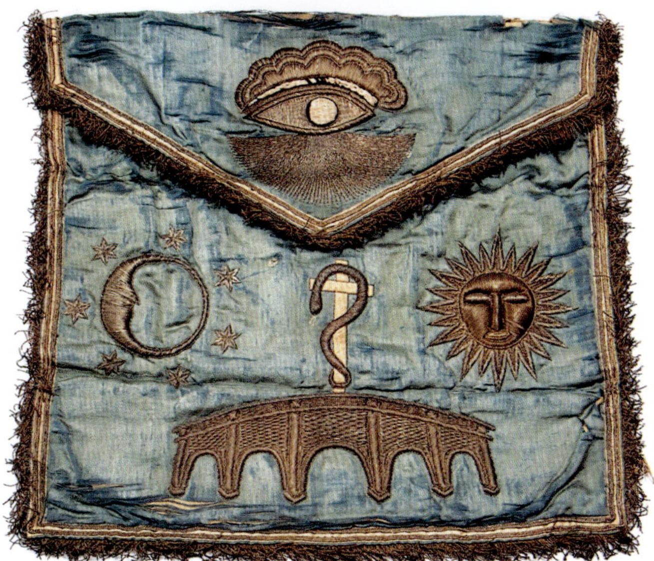

Voting on Membership

The museum has three ballot boxes. These are used during lodge meetings, principally to vote on candidates for admission. The ballot is secret and all members of the lodge are entitled to vote. Usually this is done by giving each a white ball and a black ball. The white is in favour of the candidate and the black against. After the members have voted, the Worshipful Master declares the result.

This system of black and white balls has resulted in the phrase 'being blackballed' entering into the English language. Indeed, there are several phrases in common use that have masonic origins. These include 'a square deal,' being 'on the level' and being 'put through the third degree.'

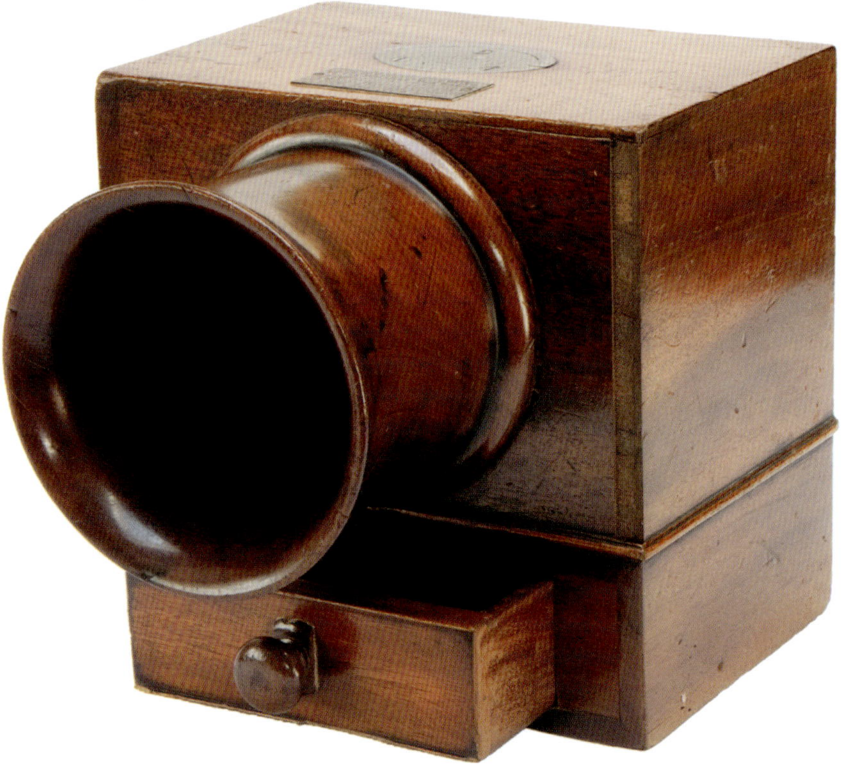

Ballot box. To vote, members put a black or white ball through the funnel and it drops into the drawer below.

United Grand Lodge of England

English freemasonry is governed by the United Grand Lodge of England, with the Grand Master at the head of the whole Order. The headquarters is at Freemasons' Hall in London. There are about 8,000 Craft lodges under its jurisdiction, organised mostly through provinces in England and Wales. A province usually consists of a single historic county as they were before 1965. Hence we still have a province of Middlesex and a province of Cumberland and Westmorland. Lancashire, Yorkshire and Kent are divided into two provinces.

The foundation stone of Freemasons' Hall was laid in 1927 and dedicated to those who died in World War I. It was financed by subscription and those masons who donated to its building were presented with the special jewel below.

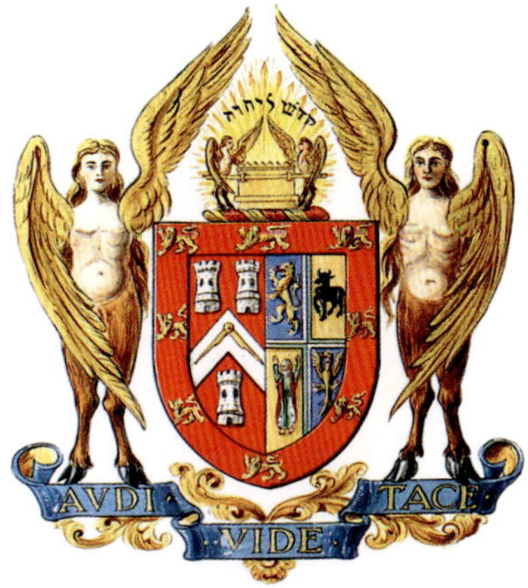

Arms of the United Grand Lodge of England.

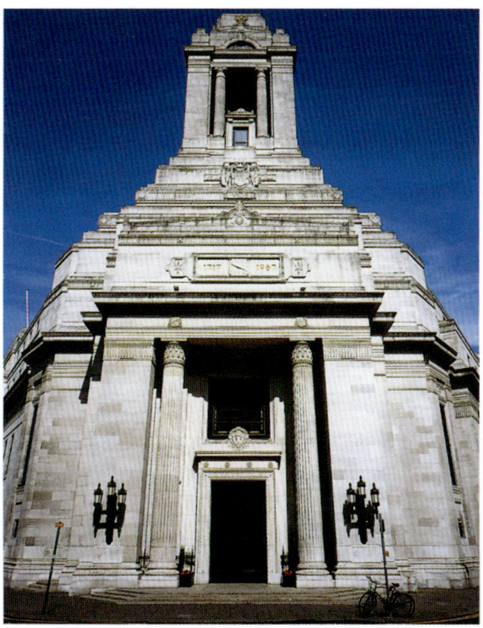

Freemasons' Hall in Great Queen Street.

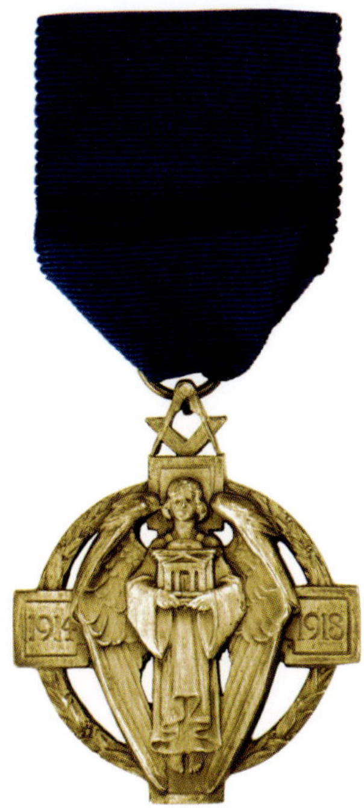

Masonic Million Memorial Fund Commemorative Jewel, in the form of a cross to signify sacrifice.

Freemasonry in Kent

There are approximately 300 masonic lodges in Kent, meeting in 34 masonic temples in East Kent and 11 in West Kent. Therefore several masonic lodges may meet at one masonic temple at different times.

Grand Lodges, provinces and individual lodges have a team of officers, such as a Treasurer, Secretary and Director of Ceremonies. All wear different regalia.

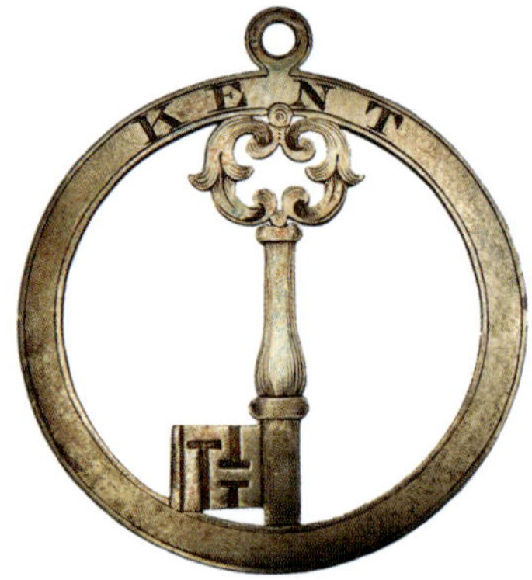

ABOVE: **Collar jewel** for the Provincial Treasurer for Kent, dated 1904. His symbol is a key.

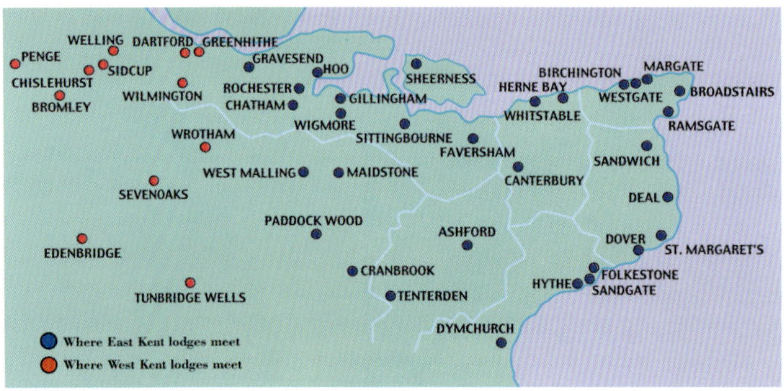

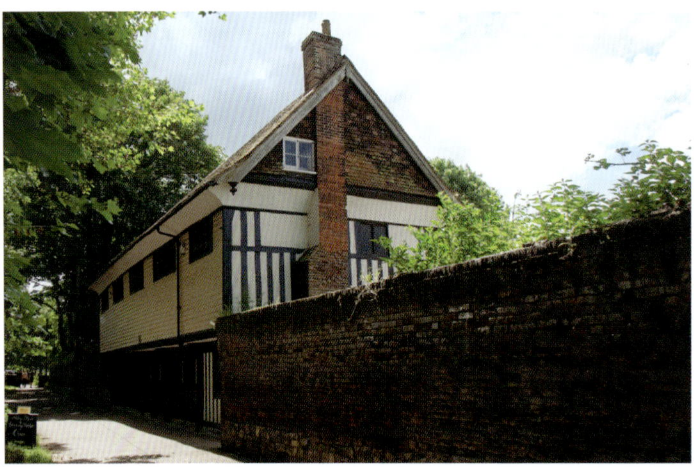

BELOW: **Collar jewel** showing the 'Invicta' prancing horse, the symbol of Kent, between two pillars in an irradiated circle. The purpose of the jewel is uncertain but it has been adopted as the museum's logo.

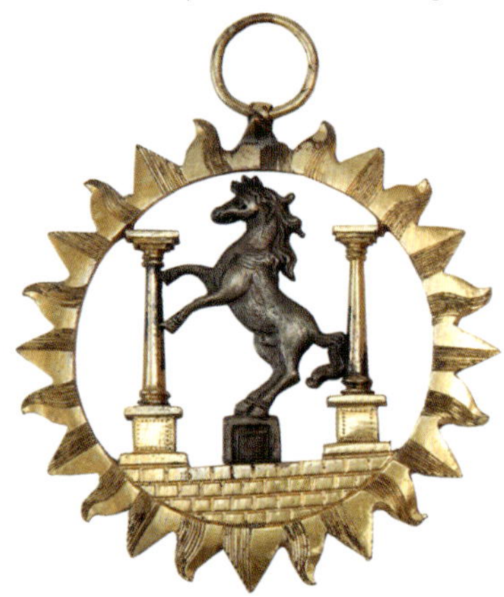

LEFT: The **Masonic Hall** in Faversham is probably the most beautiful in Kent. Built as a grammar school in 1587, it was purchased by the masons in 1887. The school room is now the temple. Downstairs is the refectory where the lodge members dine after a meeting.

Cornwallis Family

MUCH OF THE HISTORY of Freemasonry in Kent is associated with the Cornwallis family. Several of their portraits can be seen on display.

Colonel Fiennes Cornwallis, the first Baron Cornwallis of Linton, was Provincial Grand Master for Kent from 1905 to 1935, as well as Deputy Grand Master of the United Grand Lodge of England. He opened this museum in 1933 to house a large collection of masonic artefacts.

Colonel Fiennes Cornwallis (1864–1935), the first Baron Cornwallis of Linton.

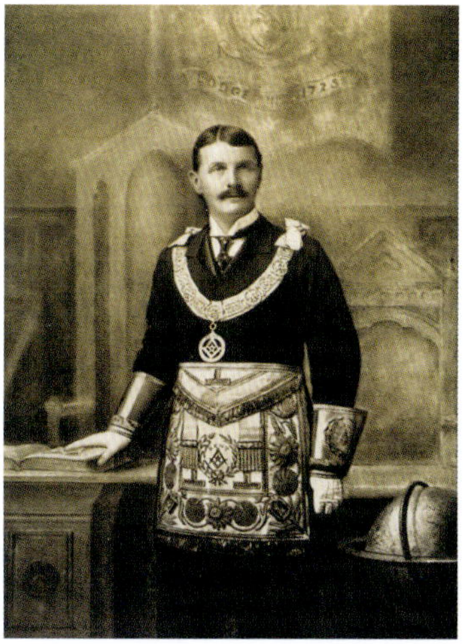

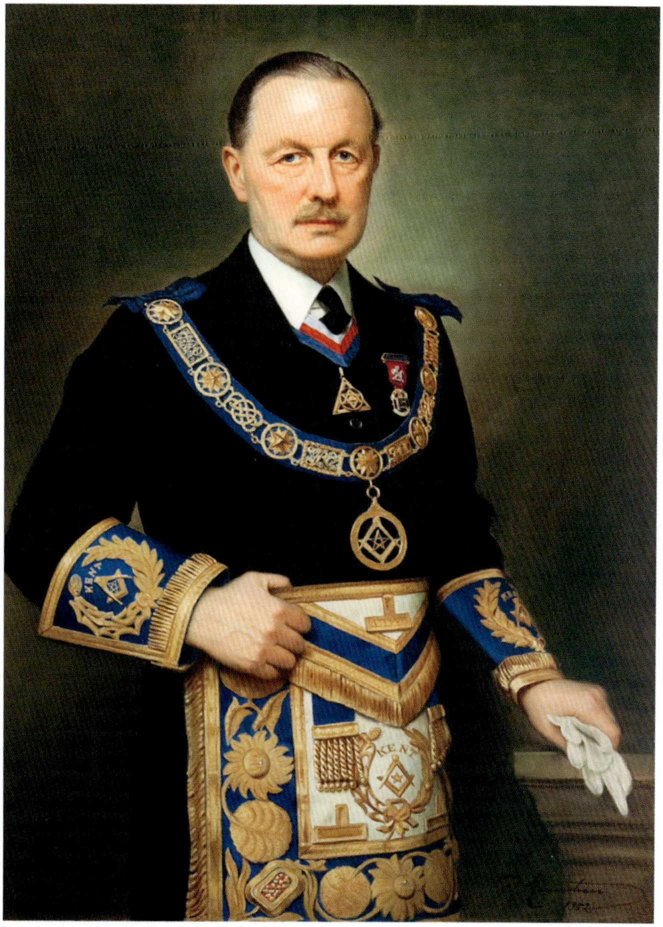

At that time the Grand Lodge building in London was being rebuilt, so Lord Cornwallis was able to obtain the inner doors and the stained glass windows (see page 1).

Portrait of **the second Baron Cornwallis** (1892–1982).

The Cornwallis family has been generous in donating many items. One of the display cabinets is made up entirely of items from them.

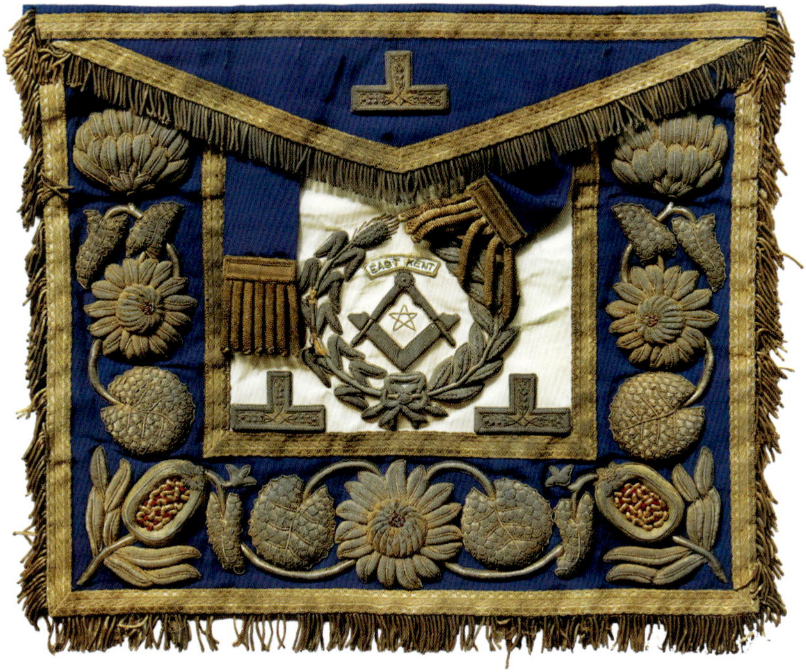

LEFT: **Lord Cornwallis's apron** as Provincial Grand Master.

BELOW LEFT: **Escritoire**, or writing box, presented to Lord Cornwallis by the British India Association in Calcutta (now Kolkata) in 1927.

BELOW RIGHT: **Japanese box** inlaid with masonic symbols and dated about 1870.

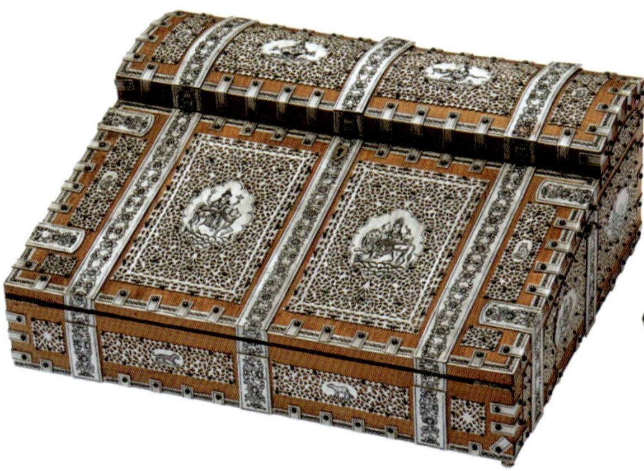

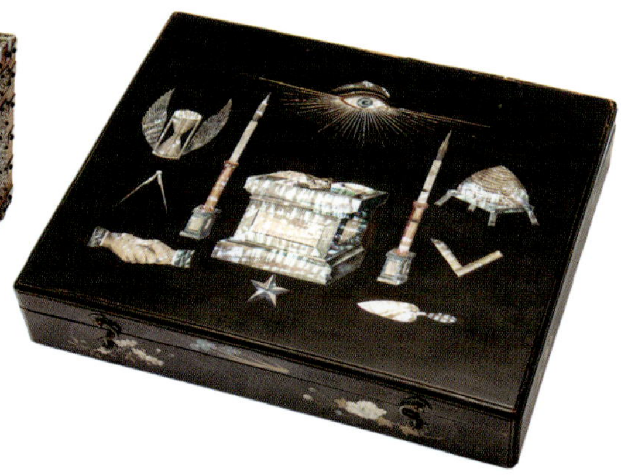

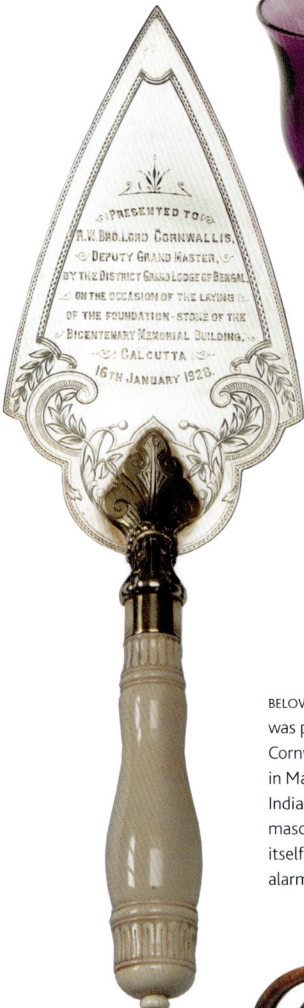

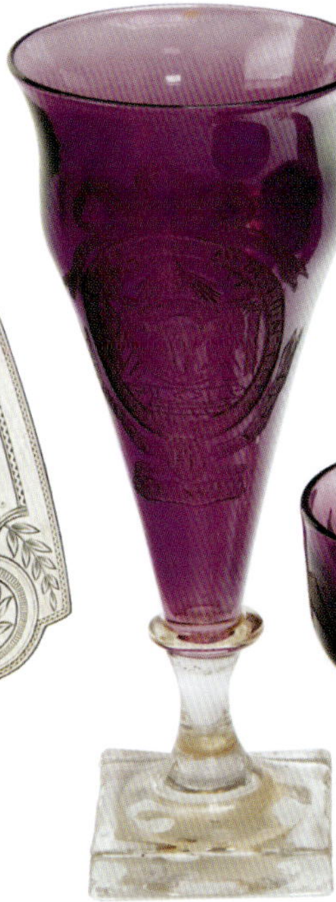

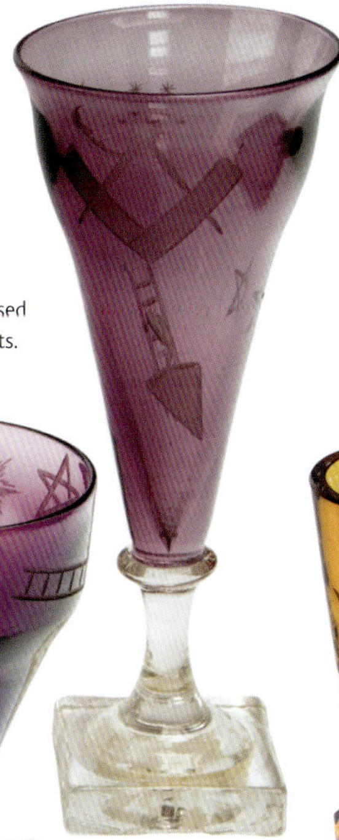

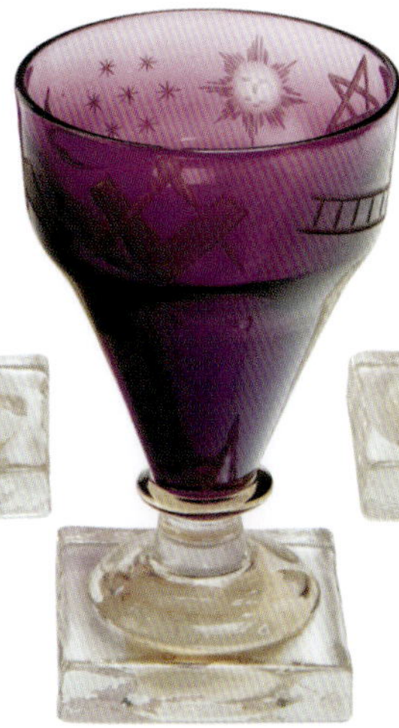

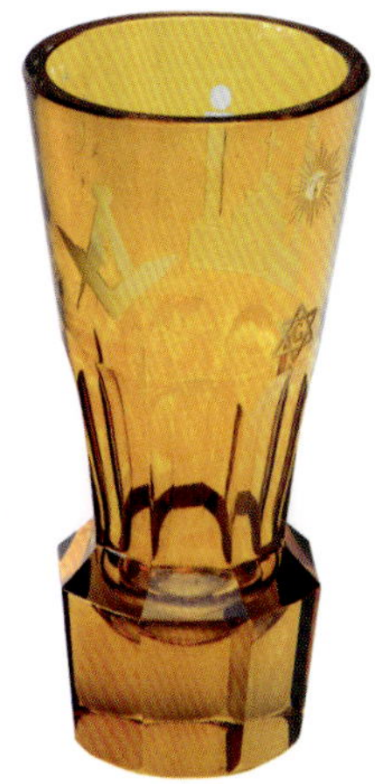

Firing glasses, used for making toasts.

BELOW: This **ornate clock** was presented to Lord Cornwallis while he was in Madras (now Chennai), India, in 1978 by the masons there. The clock itself is a Westclox alarm clock.

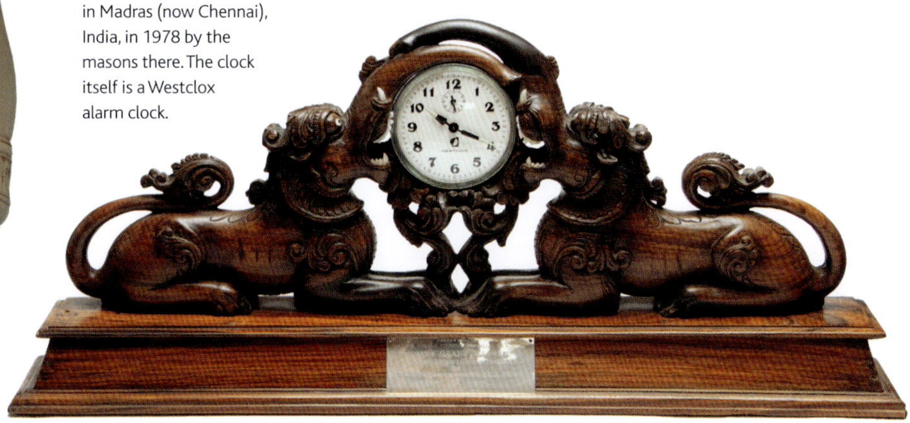

ABOVE: **Trowel** presented to Lord Cornwallis in Calcutta in 1928.

Lodge Officers

This plan shows how the officers of a masonic lodge are seated in the temple. The Worshipful Master sits at the top, known as the east, from where he conducts the ceremony. The next most senior officers are the Senior and Junior Wardens, sitting in the west and south respectively. The Secretary and Treasurer sit in the north.

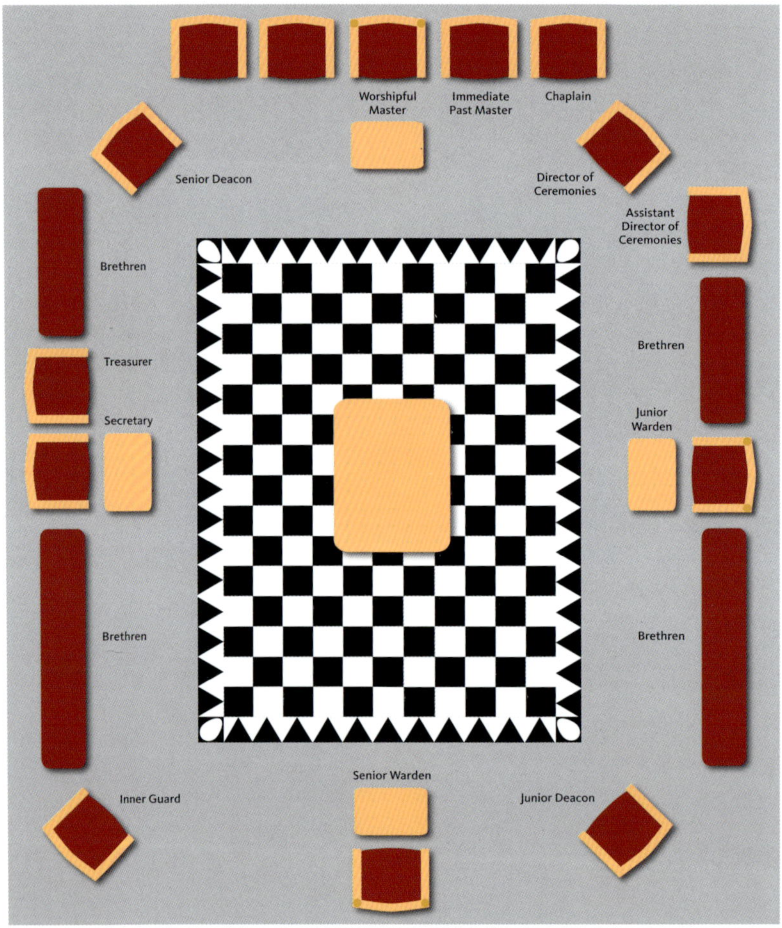

To the Worshipful Master's left are the Immediate Past Master (the previous year's Master) and to his left the Chaplain, who leads the lodge in prayer. On the floor of the lodge is the Director of Ceremonies, who ensures the ceremony is properly carried out, and the Senior and Junior Deacons, who conduct the candidates through the ceremonies. Inside the door sits the Inner Guard, who takes reports from the Tyler, who is outside the door, on any candidate or member wishing to enter the room.

What might usually be described as medals or medallions are called 'jewels' in Freemasonry. Here is a selection of officers' jewels, the insignia of office. They are attached to a light blue collar worn around the neck.

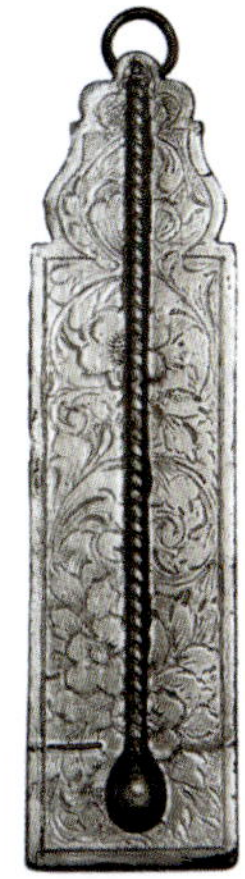

The plumb rule worn by the Junior Warden.

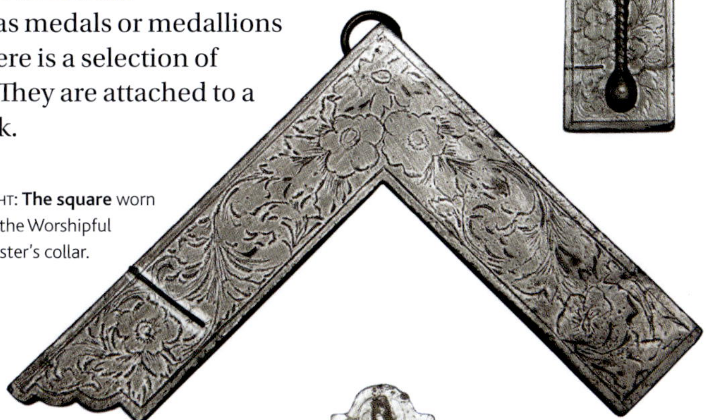

RIGHT: **The square** worn on the Worshipful Master's collar.

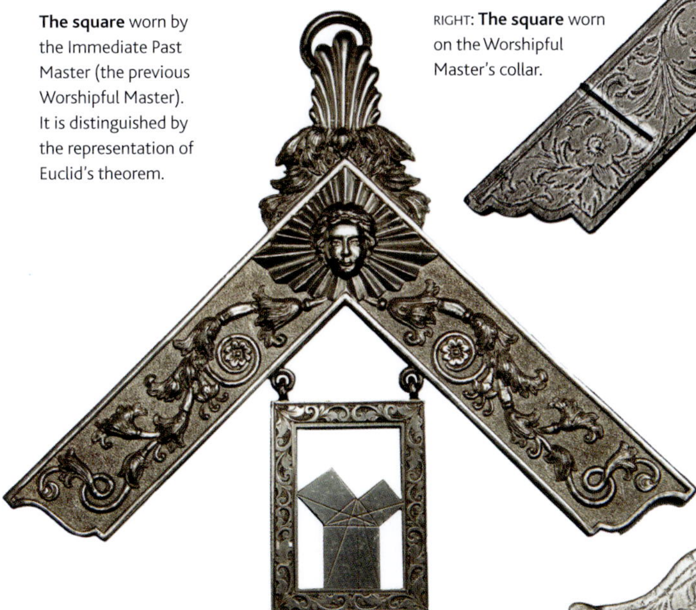

The square worn by the Immediate Past Master (the previous Worshipful Master). It is distinguished by the representation of Euclid's theorem.

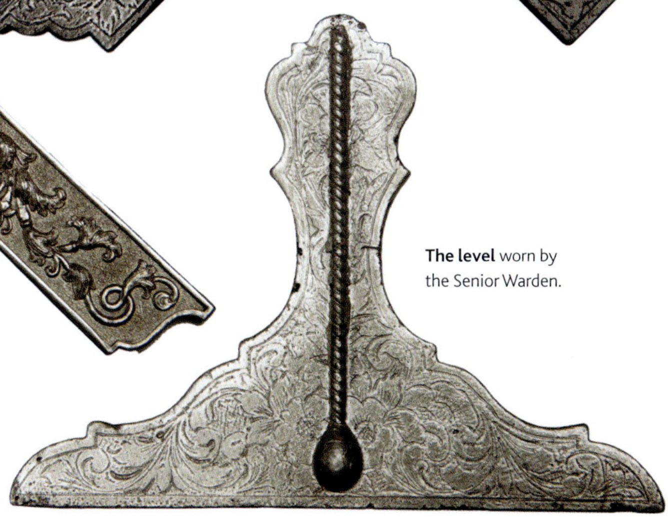

The level worn by the Senior Warden.

PAST MASTER JEWELS

ONCE A MASON has completed his term of office as Worshipful Master, he usually installs his successor in a ceremonial ritual, communicating more signs and passwords to the new Master. This giving of signs and passwords is only done as a mason progresses.

As a thank you to the outgoing Master, many lodges present him with a Past Master's jewel, which he is entitled to wear on his breast pocket when he attends future meetings. Here are some from lodges around Kent. More can be viewed on request.

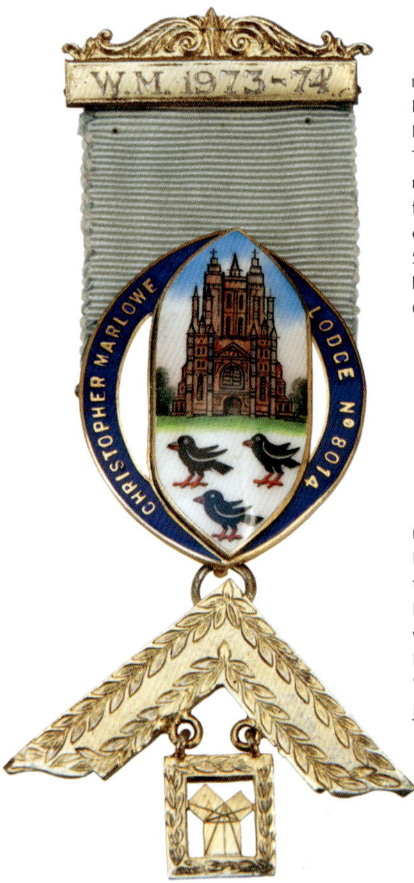

LEFT: Christopher Marlowe Lodge No.8014, Canterbury. This lodge was named after the famous playwright, contemporary of Shakespeare, who was baptised at St George's Church, Canterbury.

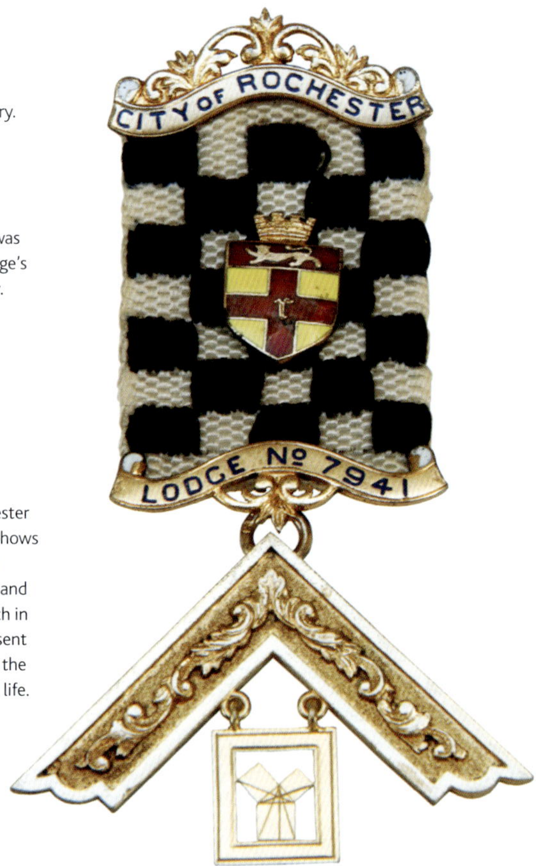

RIGHT: City of Rochester Lodge No.7941. It shows the coat of arms of Rochester on black and white squares, which in Freemasonry represent 'opposites', such as the joys and sorrows of life.

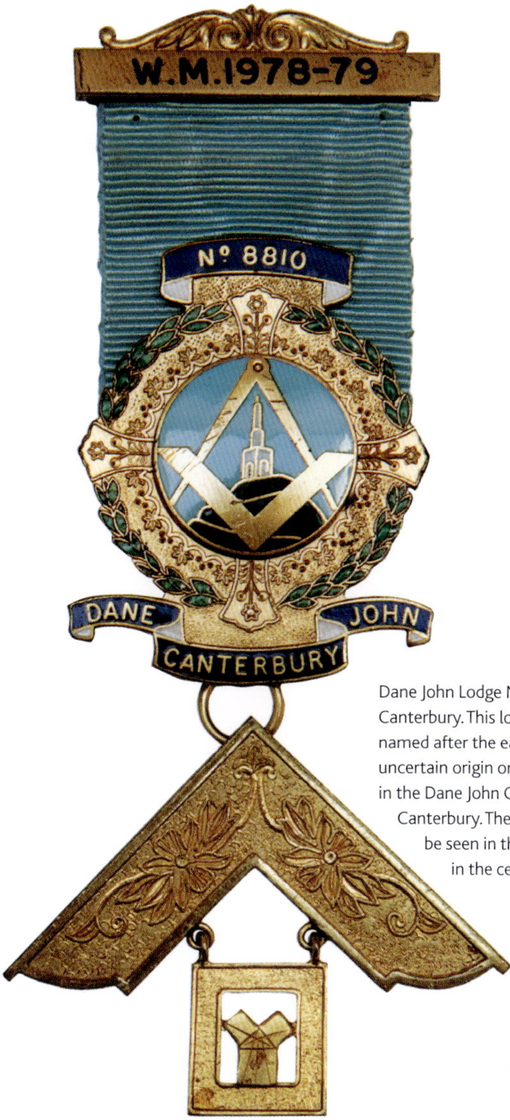

Dane John Lodge No.8810, Canterbury. This lodge was named after the earthwork of uncertain origin or purpose in the Dane John Gardens, Canterbury. The mound can be seen in the enamelling in the centre.

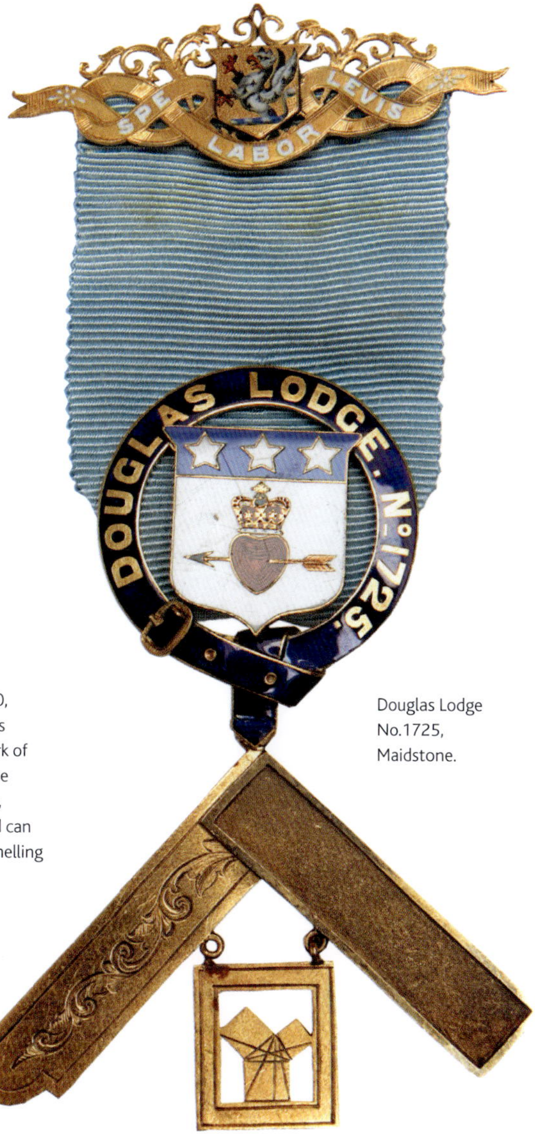

Douglas Lodge No.1725, Maidstone.

Holy Royal Arch

In 'craft' lodges, the masonic rituals and ceremonies are based around the story of the building of King Solomon's temple at Jerusalem. After a mason has taken his Third Degree in the Craft, he becomes eligible to join another Degree, the Holy Royal Arch, sometimes known simply as the 'Chapter'. The story in the Chapter advances the story of King Solomon's temple by nearly 500 years, when the original temple had been destroyed and certain discoveries were made during the rebuilding.

There have been chapters in Kent since the eighteenth century. Chapters are held

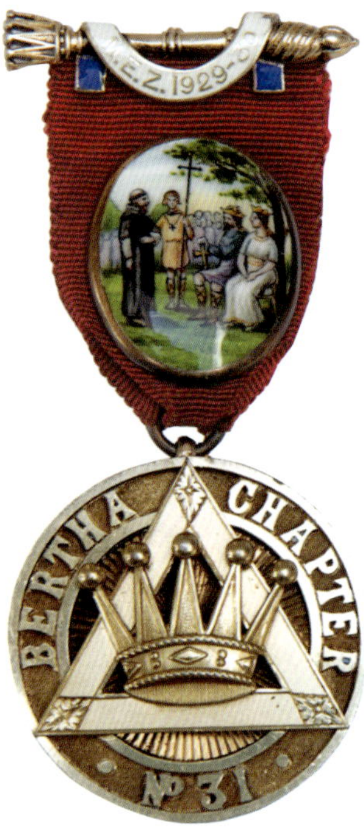

Past Principal's jewel from Bertha Chapter No.31, dated 1929–30. The enamelled picture in the centre shows St Augustine arriving in Kent in AD 597 and meeting King Ethelbert of Kent and Queen Bertha under an oak tree.

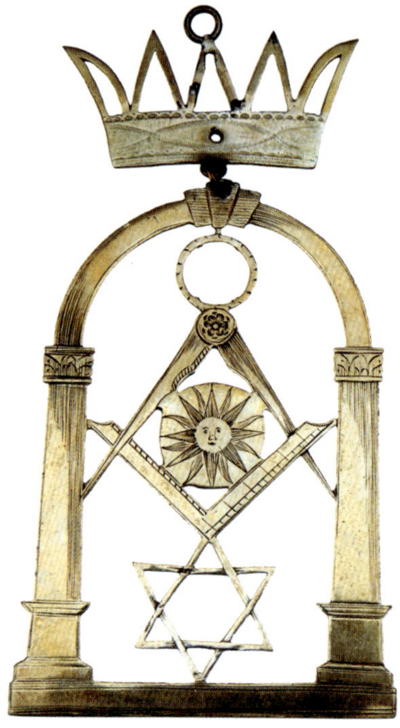

This **jewel** came from the Concord Chapter No.38, which no longer exists but met in Canterbury from 1783. It is now worn in Bertha Chapter No.31, Canterbury.

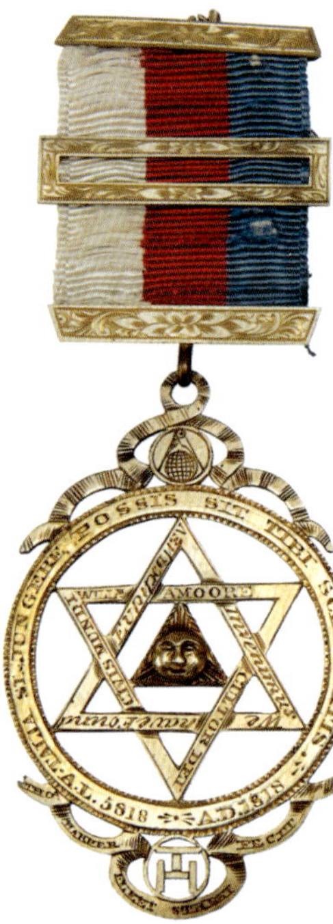

A **chapter jewel** made in 1818 by the eminent silversmith Thomas Harper. He was initiated into Freemasonry in Bristol and became involved in the Holy Royal Arch in the 1770s. The museum has several of his jewels, which are highly sought after.

separately from lodges, with different officers and different regalia. Instead of being called 'Brother,' as he was in the Craft lodge, the new member is now called a 'Companion.' The Worshipful Master of the lodge here is called the First Principal.

All companions wear an apron and a sash 'indented in red and blue,' together with a breast jewel. The colour of the ribbon on the jewel depends on the companion's rank. Grand Officers and Provincial Grand Officers also wear a collar.

Here are several chapter jewels, worn on the left breast like a medal.

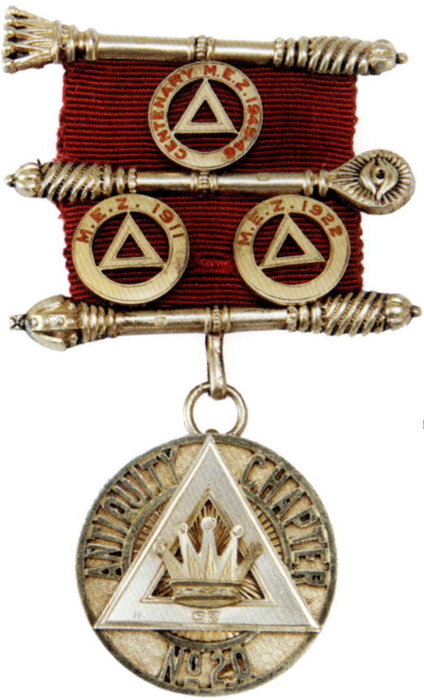

This **Past Principal's jewel** from Kent Royal Arch Chapter of Antiquity No.20, Chatham, shows miniatures of the three sceptres carried by the three principal officers of a chapter during a ceremony. The sceptre tops differ – there is a crown, an irradiated eye and a mitre.

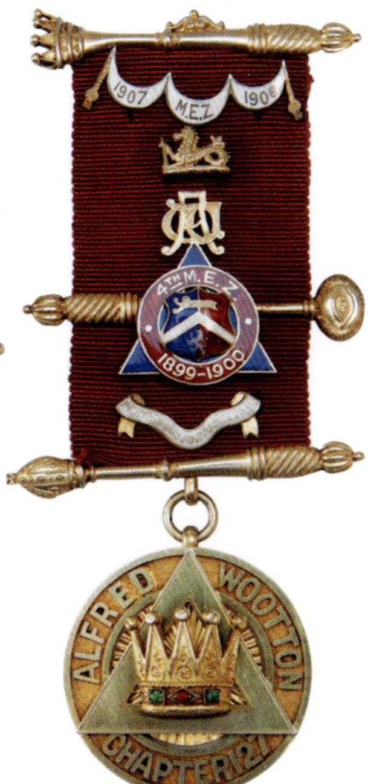

A similar **Past Principal's jewel** from the Alfred Wootton Chapter No.127, Margate, dated 1907.

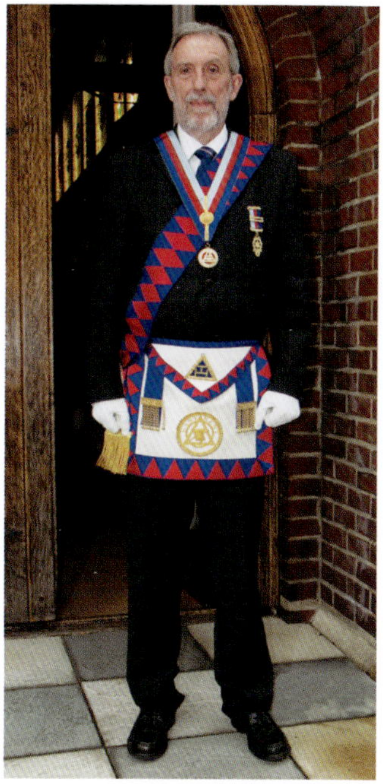

Museum curator Tony Periton wearing the **regalia** of a Provincial Grand Chapter Officer.

Other Masonic Orders

As well as the Holy Royal Arch, a mason who has taken his Third Degree in the Craft may, if he wishes, join other masonic Orders. The Orders are shown on the family tree opposite. A more complex version is on display in the museum.

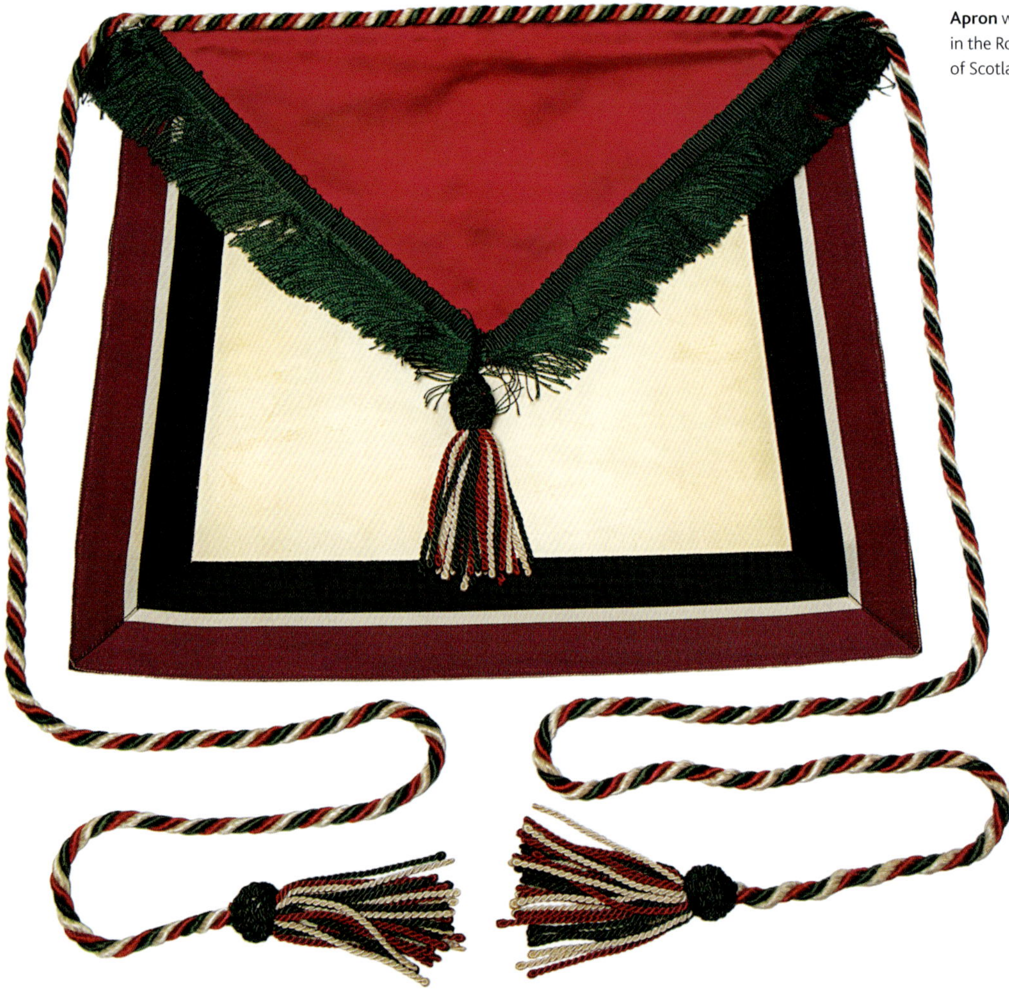

Apron worn in the Royal Order of Scotland.

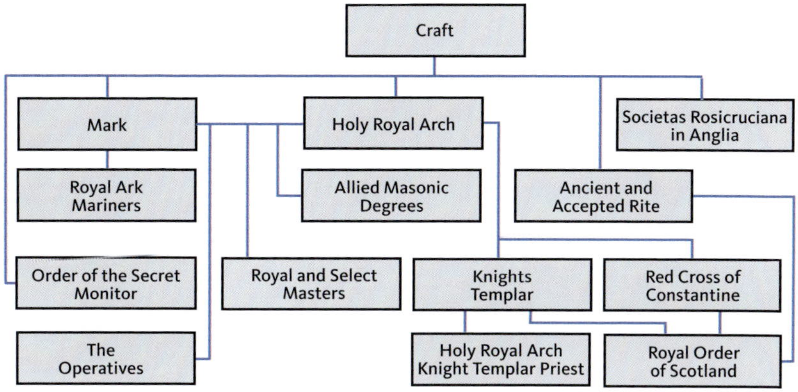

A family tree showing the other Orders of Freemasonry. It shows the progress a mason may make from the Craft lodges. For example, to be admitted to the Red Cross of Constantine, a Master Mason must be a member of the Holy Royal Arch.

The principal Orders are the Mark, Royal Ark Mariner, Knights Templar, Rose Croix (otherwise called the Ancient and Accepted Rite), Red Cross of Constantine, Royal and Select Masters, the Allied Masonic Degrees, Order of the Secret Monitor, Knight Templar Priests and Royal Order of Scotland.

Although the Craft and many of the other Orders are open to men of all faiths some, including Knights Templar, Rose Croix and Red Cross of Constantine, do require a Christian faith to be eligible for membership.

BELOW LEFT: **Apron** formerly worn by an eighteenth-Degree mason of the Rose Croix.

BELOW: **Knight Templar apron**. These are no longer worn.

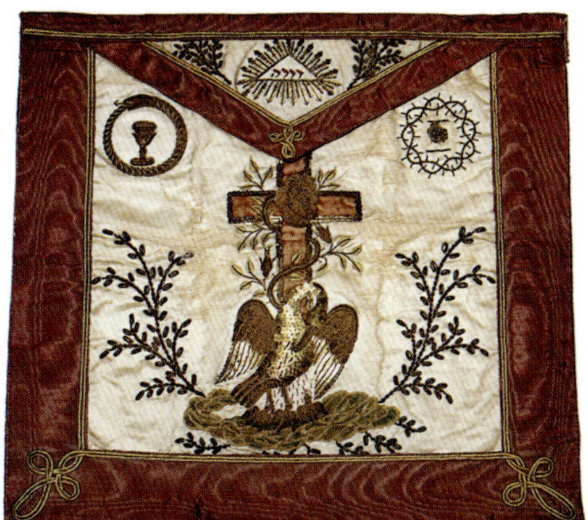

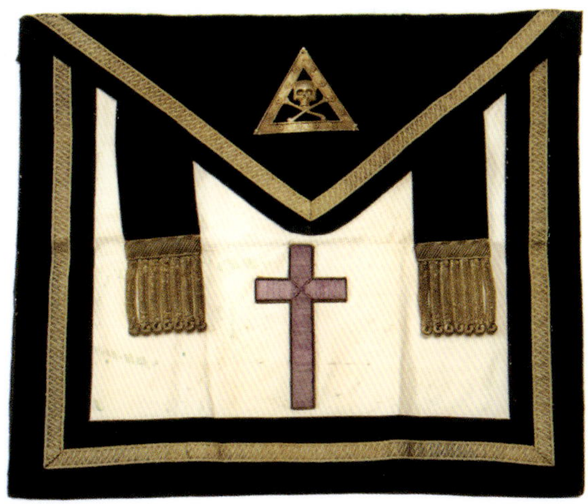

Each Order has its own hierarchy, system of Degrees and secrets, and very often quite elaborate regalia. Here are some examples of breast jewels.

RIGHT: **Order of the Royal Ark Mariners.**

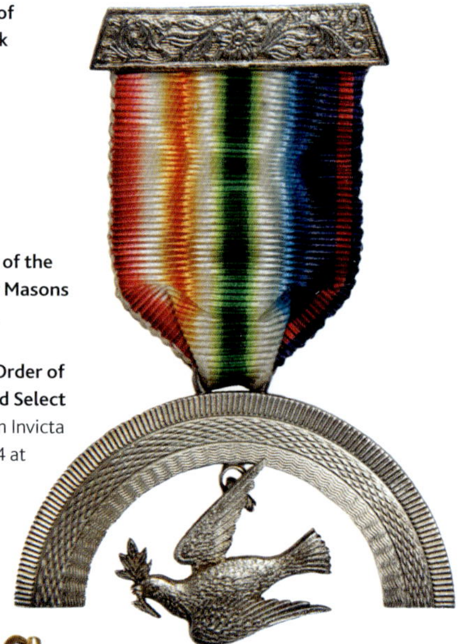

BELOW AND RIGHT: **Order of the Red Cross of Constantine** (worn together).

BELOW: **Order of the Mark Master Masons – 'The Mark'.**

BELOW RIGHT: **Order of the Royal and Select Masters**, from Invicta Council No.14 at Canterbury.

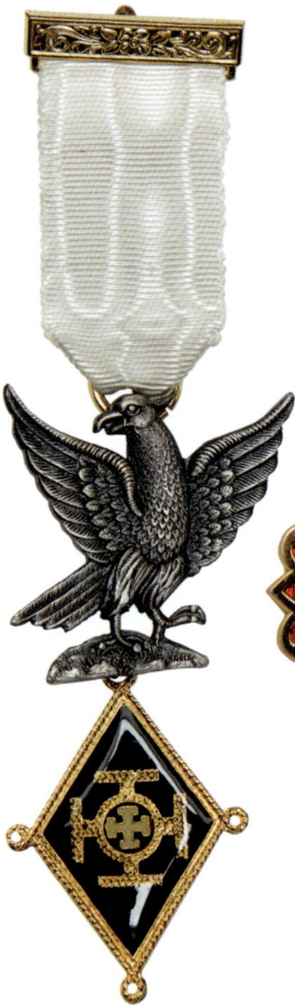

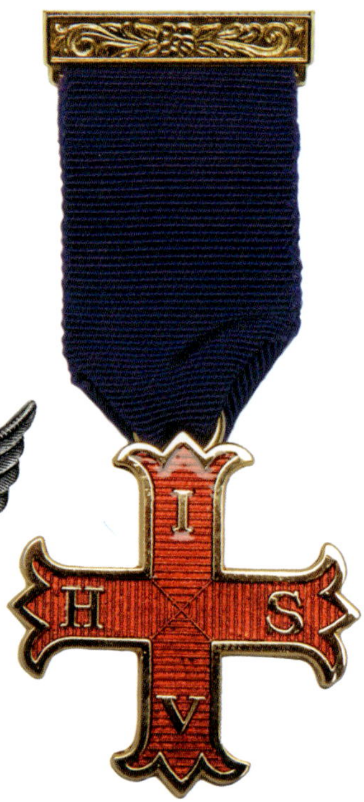

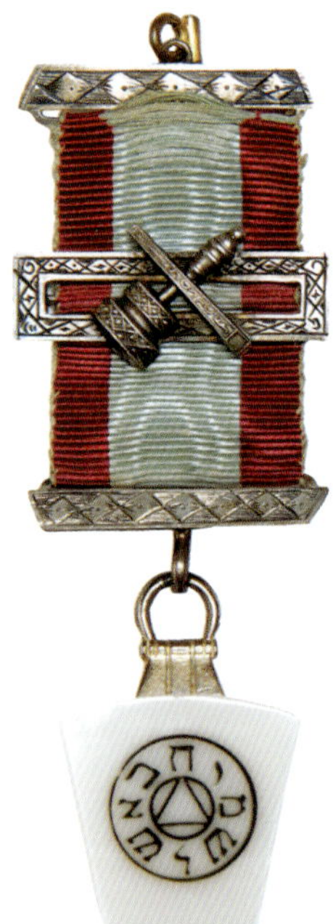

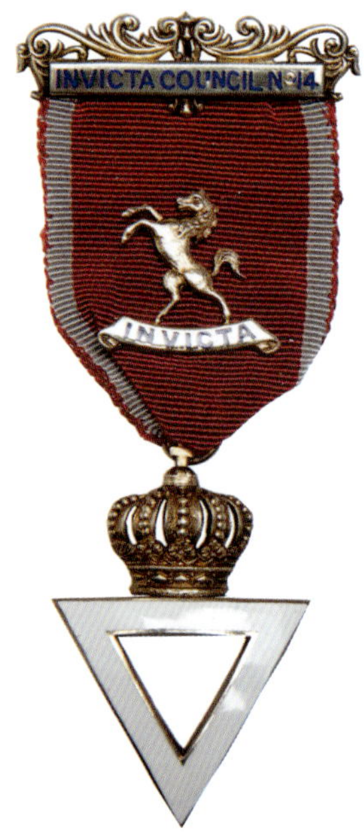

Knights Templar

The masonic Order of the Knights Templar (together with the Knights of Malta) has long held a fascination, on account of the history and legends associated with it.

The original Knights Templar were founded to guard pilgrims after the Christian Crusaders captured the Holy Land in AD 1099. They were granted land on the site of King Solomon's temple. The Templar Order was dissolved by the Pope in AD 1312.

The masonic Order of Knights Templar has no claim to a direct descent from the original Order, although many people think modern Freemasonry was influenced not only by operative stonemasons of the Middle Ages but also Knights Templar.

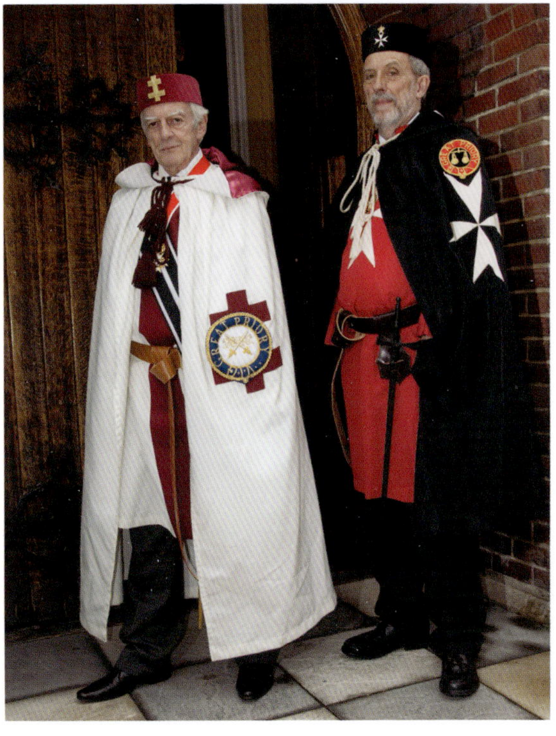

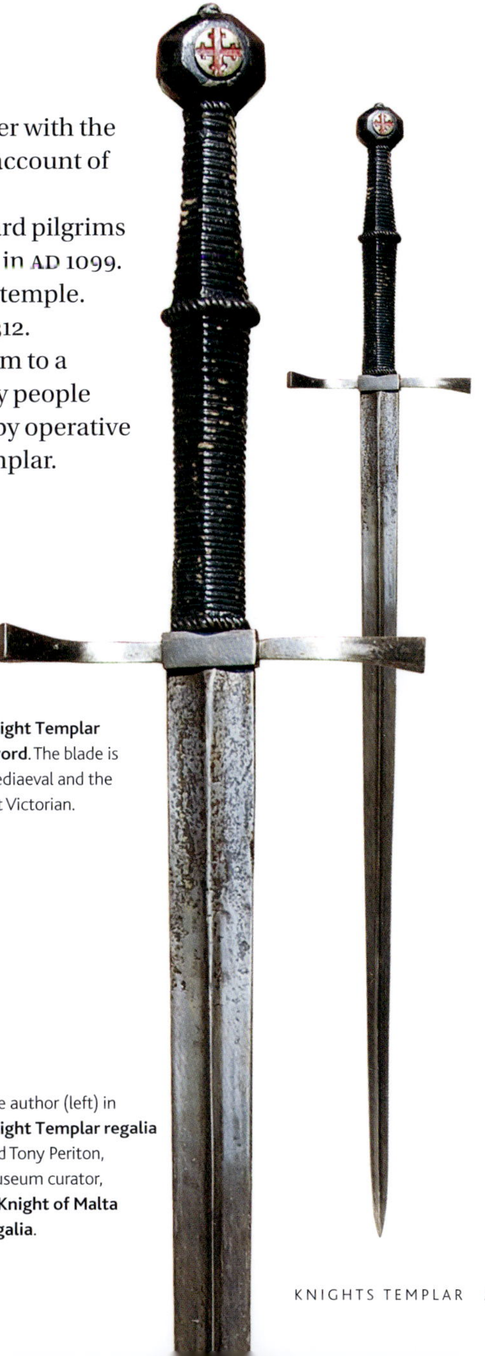

Knight Templar sword. The blade is mediaeval and the hilt Victorian.

The author (left) in **Knight Templar regalia** and Tony Periton, museum curator, in **Knight of Malta regalia**.

MASONIC CHARITY

ONE IMPORTANT ASPECT of Freemasonry is charity. In Britain Freemasonry is the largest giver of money to charity after the National Lottery.

Money is raised *only* from Freemasons and their friends. It is never raised from non-masonic sources, such as street collections.

Freemasonry has four charities of its own.

1. The Freemasons' Grand Charity
2. The Royal Masonic Trust for Girls and Boys
3. The Royal Masonic Benevolent Institution
4. The Masonic Samaritan Fund

Every so often a province holds a 'Festival', typically over four to seven years, to raise funds for masonic charity. In the 2014 Festival, the Province of East Kent raised £3.6 million for the Grand Charity.

Grand Lodge, Provincial Grand Lodge and individual lodges donate money to both national and local charities. Examples might be an international disaster such as the earthquake in Haiti, to a local hospice or the Guide Dogs. In East Kent we have supported apprentice stonemasons at Canterbury Cathedral.

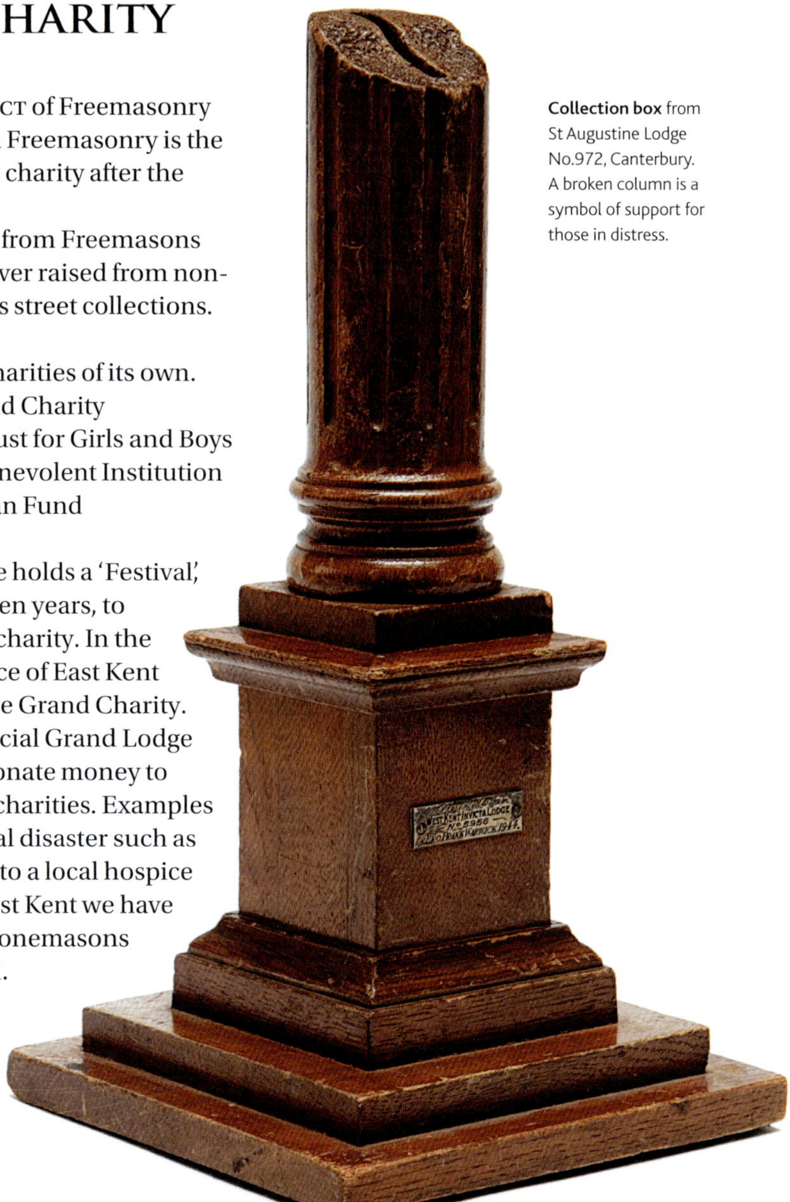

Collection box from St Augustine Lodge No.972, Canterbury. A broken column is a symbol of support for those in distress.

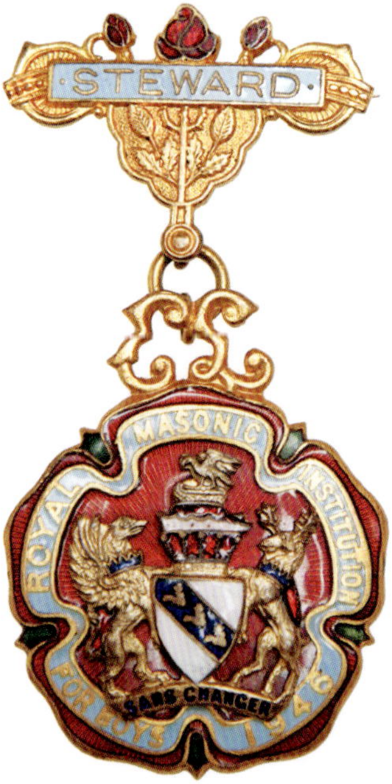

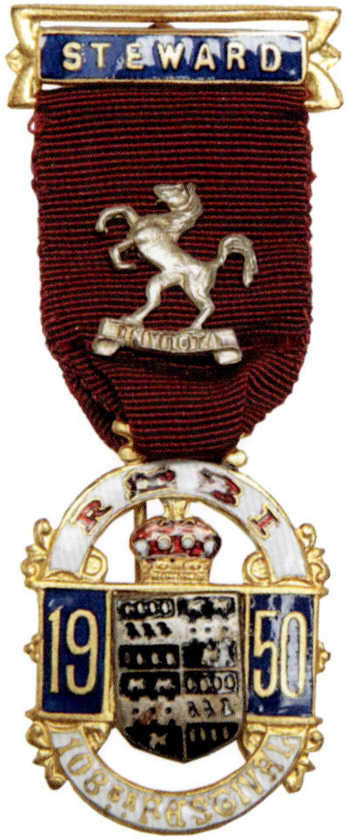

BELOW: **Charity jewel** for the 2014 East Kent Festival. The centre shows Geoffrey Chaucer, author of *The Canterbury Tales*, Rochester Castle and the Pharos (Roman Lighthouse at Dover). It is the logo for the Province of East Kent.

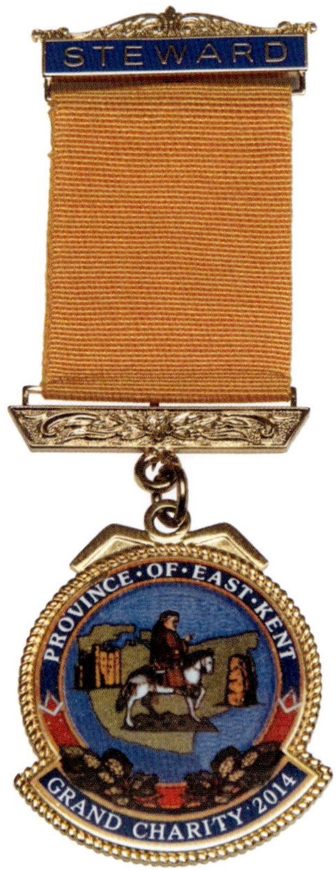

ABOVE AND RIGHT: **Breast jewels** awarded to masons for their financial contributions towards Festivals.

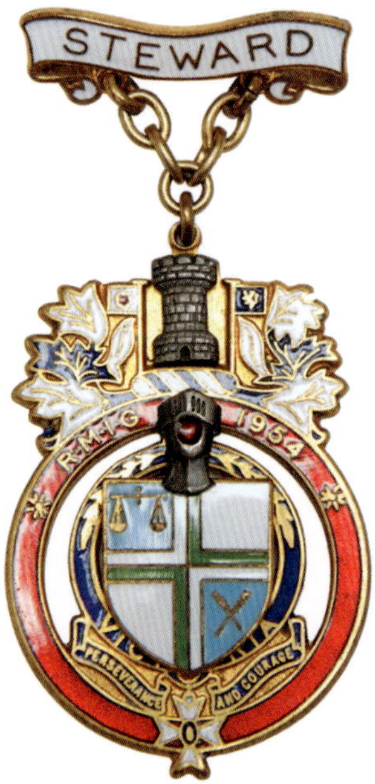

Masonic Dining

A TYPICAL MASONIC LODGE meets in the late afternoon or early evening. Depending on the ceremony being performed, the meeting lasts for a couple of hours. Most meetings are followed by a formal dinner, at which the Worshipful Master presides. The meal is followed by a number of toasts. The first is always to the Queen, followed by the Grand Master. Others include a toast to the Worshipful Master, to a candidate when he is initiated (first admitted to Freemasonry) and to the visitors. Many toasts require a response by the recipient.

Often the toasts involve making a lot of noise by hand claps and banging on the dining table. Traditionally this was done with a firing glass, hence some drinking glasses displayed in the museum have thick glass bottoms so they would not break.

The formality of the dinner has led to individual lodges obtaining their own tableware, glassware, jugs for beer and water, decanters and fruit bowls.

Today firing glasses and other items are produced to commemorate significant events, such as a lodge celebrating its centenary, and given out as souvenirs.

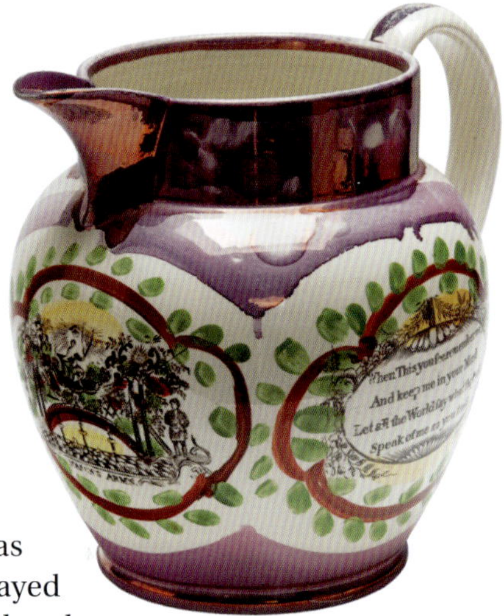

Sunderland ware jug with masonic verses.

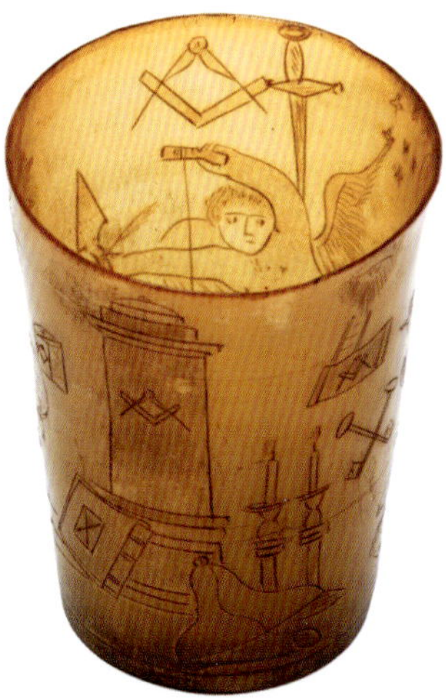

Horn beaker with masonic symbols, possibly eighteenth century.

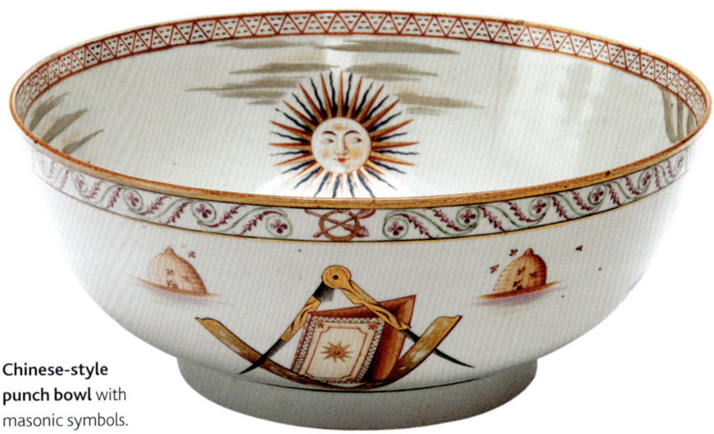

Chinese-style punch bowl with masonic symbols.

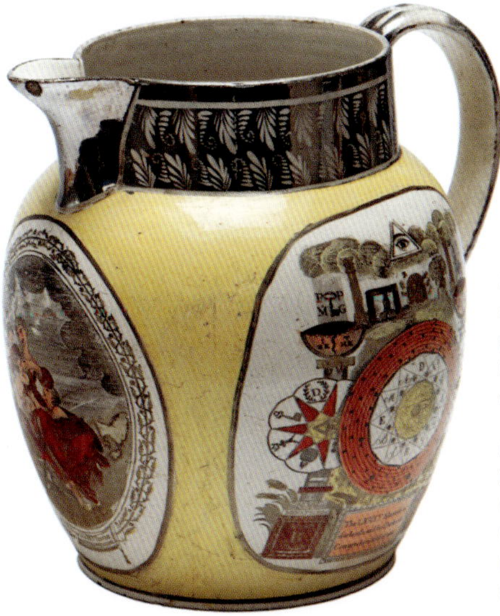

LEFT: **Newcastle canary-and-silver glazed jug** with masonic symbols and verse.

RIGHT: **Large two-handled jug** from Halfway House, Challock, near Ashford. It measures 13 inches (33cm) in height.

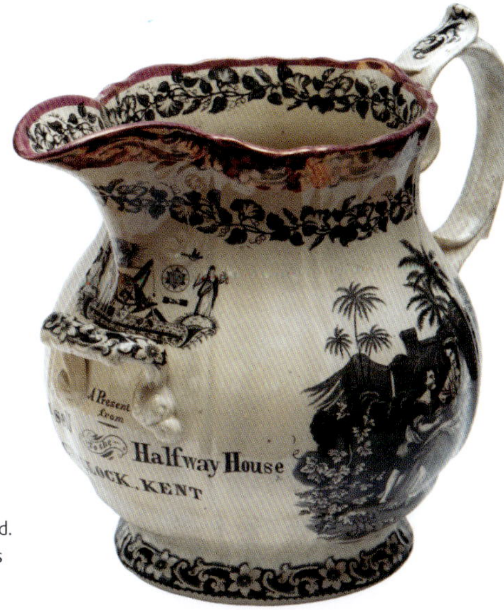

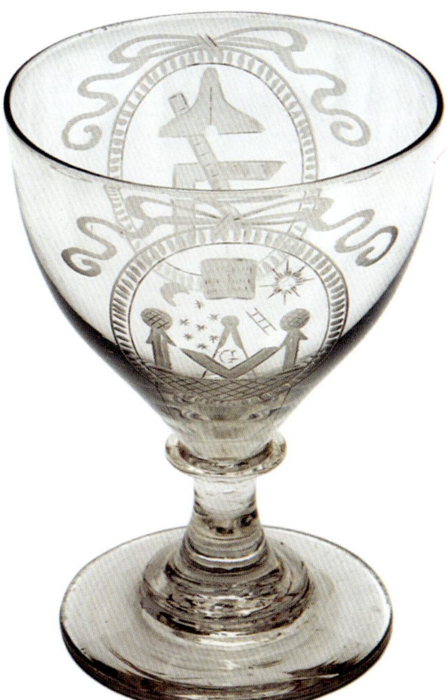

LEFT: **Glass goblet** engraved with square and compasses, Bible, pillars and other masonic symbols.

RIGHT: **Red firing glass** from the Cornwallis collection.

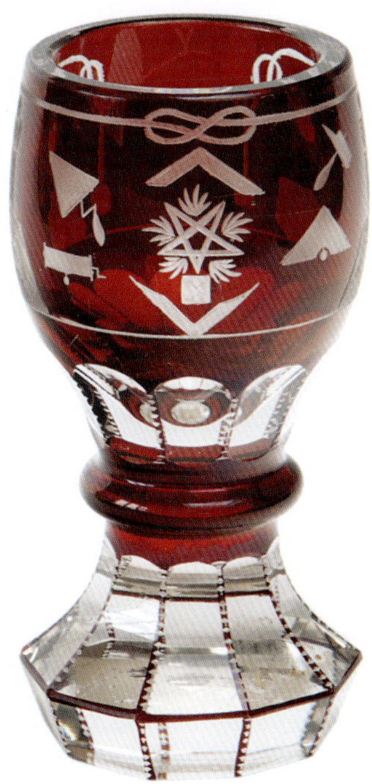

Freemasonry and the Armed Services

Kent has always been at the forefront of the defence of Britain, so many towns in the county have a naval or military connection. Among these are Chatham, Sheerness, Deal, Dover and Canterbury. Many masonic lodges admitted members exclusively from the Armed Services. Army regiments had their own lodges and as they were posted around the world, the lodge went with them. They would continue to have meetings and had a 'travelling box' containing all the equipment, or 'furniture', needed to conduct the ceremonies.

Since the end of World War II the size of the Armed Services has shrunk and Chatham and Sheerness dockyards have closed. Many of the naval and military lodges have disappeared but 15 or so still survive in Kent, although membership is no longer exclusively naval or military. Examples are the Union Waterloo Lodge No.13 at Dartford, which dates from 1761; the Royal Navy Lodge No.429 at Ramsgate, dating from 1835; the Royal Military Lodge No.1449 at Canterbury of 1873; and the Ordnance Lodge No.2399, whose Ladies' Festival brochure appears on page 28.

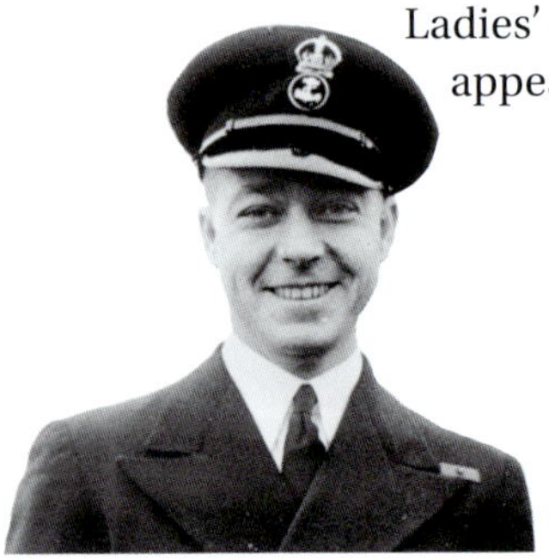

LEFT: Victoria Cross recipient **Tommy Gould** was a member of the Lord Charles Beresford Lodge No.2404 at Chatham, which was largely a Royal Marine lodge.

A nineteenth-century travelling box. It includes three gavels, two pillars with the terrestrial and celestial globes on the top, a length of rope, a dagger and working tools, such as the square and compasses, mallet and chisel. All these would be needed to conduct the ceremonies admitting candidates to the Three Degrees of Craft masonry.

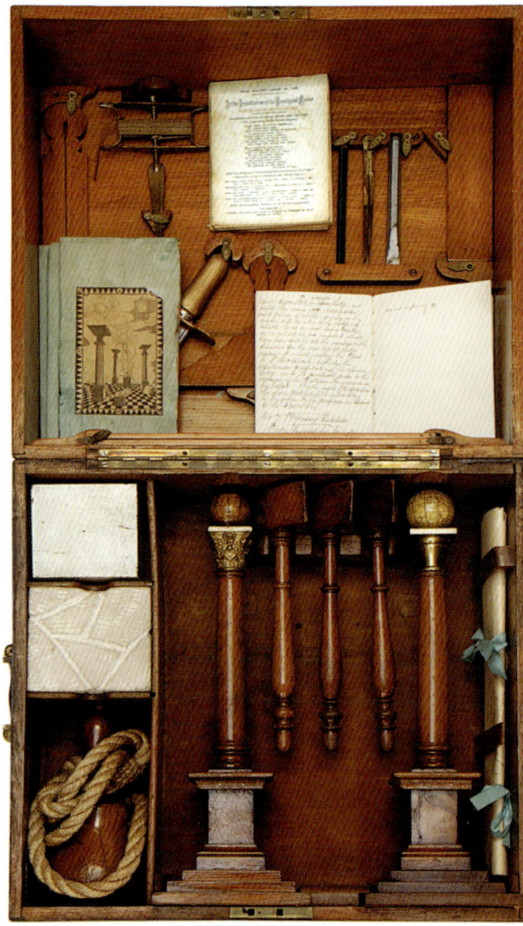

Freemasonry at War

Many Freemasons served in the Armed Services during both World Wars. The majority who lost their lives are commemorated by plaques in masonic centres around the country. Some were decorated for their valour.

Freemasons held in prisoner-of-war camps held clandestine meetings under the noses of both the Germans and Japanese. They produced the equipment needed from whatever materials were available and kept them hidden from the guards.

The Nazis in particular were anti-masonic. When the Germans occupied the Channel Islands, the masons were not permitted to meet and the masonic temple in St Helier on the island of Jersey was closed and looted. Its contents were taken back to Germany.

Had Britain been invaded and occupied in 1940, the Freemasons would have been targeted.

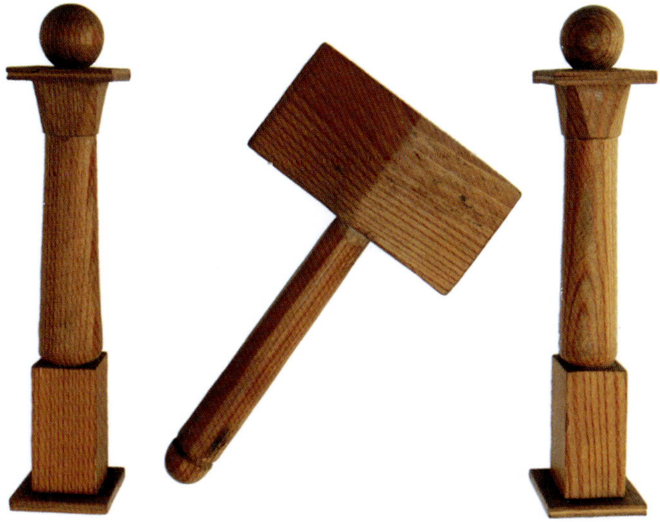

ABOVE: **Pillars and a gavel** made in a German prisoner-of-war camp in 1944.

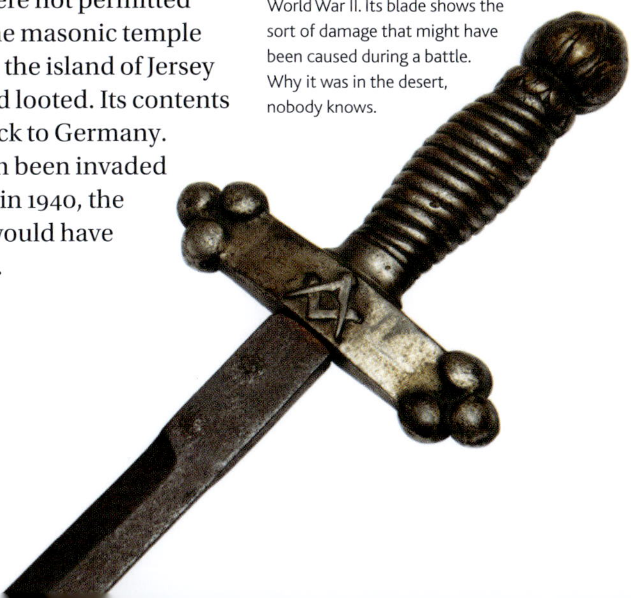

BELOW: This **sword** displays the masonic symbol of the square and compasses and was discovered in the desert sand during the North African campaign of World War II. Its blade shows the sort of damage that might have been caused during a battle. Why it was in the desert, nobody knows.

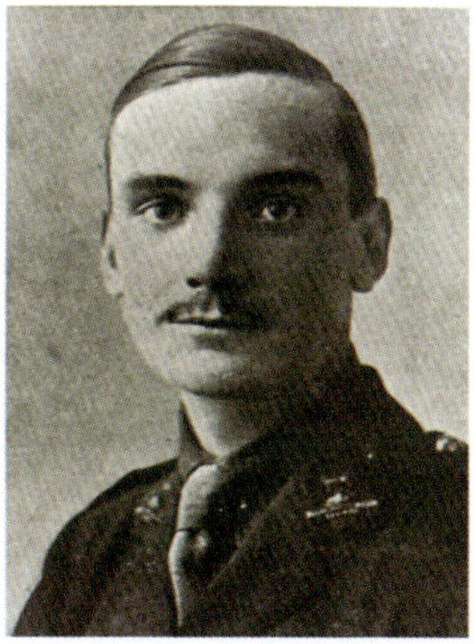

BELOW: **Lt Col Donald Dean VC**, member of St Michael's Lodge No.1273 at Sittingbourne.

Women in Freemasonry

The Freemasonry shown in this museum is limited to men in lodges under the United Grand Lodge of England. Many people do not realise that women have their own organisations – the 'Order of Woman Freemasons' and 'The Honourable Fraternity of Antient Freemasonry' – as well as their own lodges and temples.

Men and women masons never meet together for masonic meetings in a lodge. However, many lodges under the United Grand Lodge of England hold social events to which friends and family are invited. These provide an opportunity to raise money for charity by raffles and tombolas.

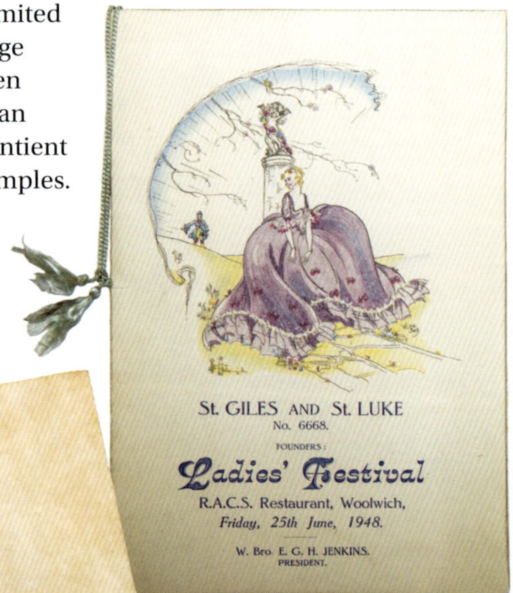

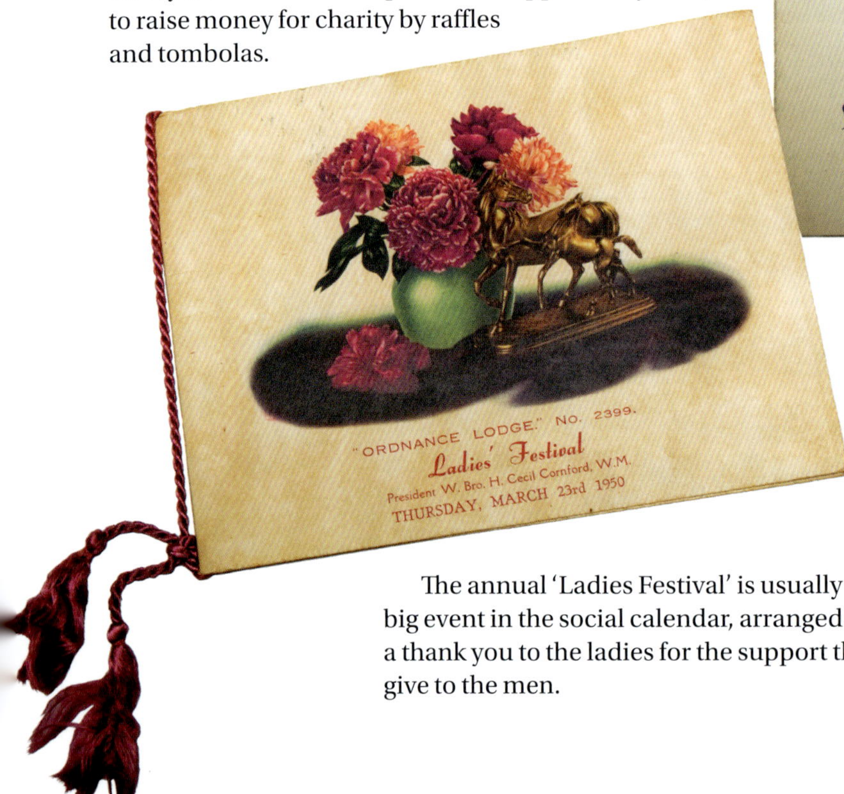

ABOVE: **Brochure** from the Ladies Festival of the Lodge of St Giles and St Mark No.6668 in 1948. Inside are the menus for the banquet, the list of toasts and the details of the entertainment, including music and singers.

LEFT: The Ladies Festival **brochure** from the Ordnance Lodge No.2399 from 1950.

The annual 'Ladies Festival' is usually the big event in the social calendar, arranged as a thank you to the ladies for the support they give to the men.

Masonry and Canterbury Cathedral

THE ORIGINS OF Freemasonry can be found in the 'operative' masons who built cathedrals, churches and castles in the Middle Ages, including Canterbury Cathedral.

Canterbury Cathedral has many points of interest concerning operative masons and also modern Freemasonry. As you walk around the Cathedral, both inside and out, you might notice little scratch marks in the stonework. Many of these are the original 'mason's marks,' made by the craftsman to identify his work. This concept of a mason's mark is carried forward to Freemasonry in one of the other Orders after the Craft – Mark masonry.

If you are in the South Quire aisle of the Cathedral, look up and you will see this **twelfth-century glass**, depicting the Queen of Sheba visiting King Solomon. She is referred to in some masonic rituals.

Some of the stained glass windows, such as this one, depict scenes that are used in modern masonic rituals. The Cathedral also has some twentieth-century stained glass windows donated by the Freemasons of Kent. If you stand in the Martyrdom, where Thomas Becket was murdered, look behind at the window with the Royal Family. It was donated in 1954.

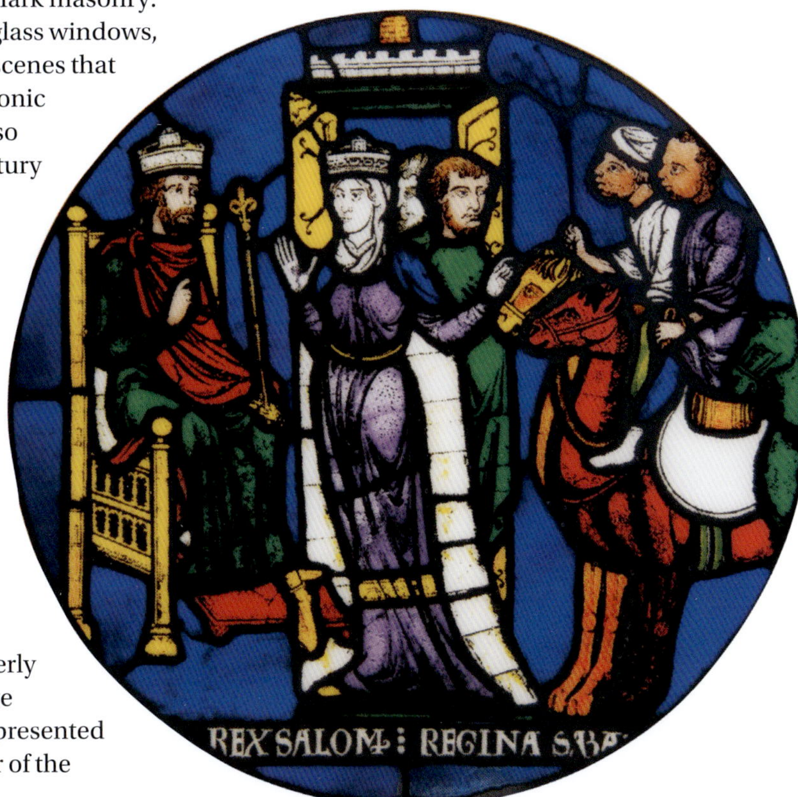

Walking through the Cloisters you will come to the Chapter House. Look inside. Masonic meetings formerly took place here. The large window facing you was presented to the Dean and Chapter of the Cathedral in 1905.

Freemasonry in Canterbury

There have been masonic lodges in Canterbury since 1730. The first met at the Red Lion tavern, next to the city's Guildhall; not the new Guildhall across the street from the museum but the original in the High Street, damaged during World War II and subsequently demolished. The site is currently a coffee house.

The Mayor and Corporation were curious about their new neighbours and evidently did not like these new-fangled Freemasons. It led to a long poem in the local newspaper condemning them.

Curiosity went further: during a masonic meeting, a lady fell through the ceiling from the room above while she was trying to listen in.

This **print of 1732** celebrates the moment the lady fell through the ceiling. The first verse says:

'The Chambermaid Moll a Girl very fat
Lay hid in the Garrett as sly as a Cat.
To find out the secrets of Masons below
Which no one can tell and themselves do not know.
Moll happen'd to slip & the ceiling broke thro.
And hung in the position you have in your view.'

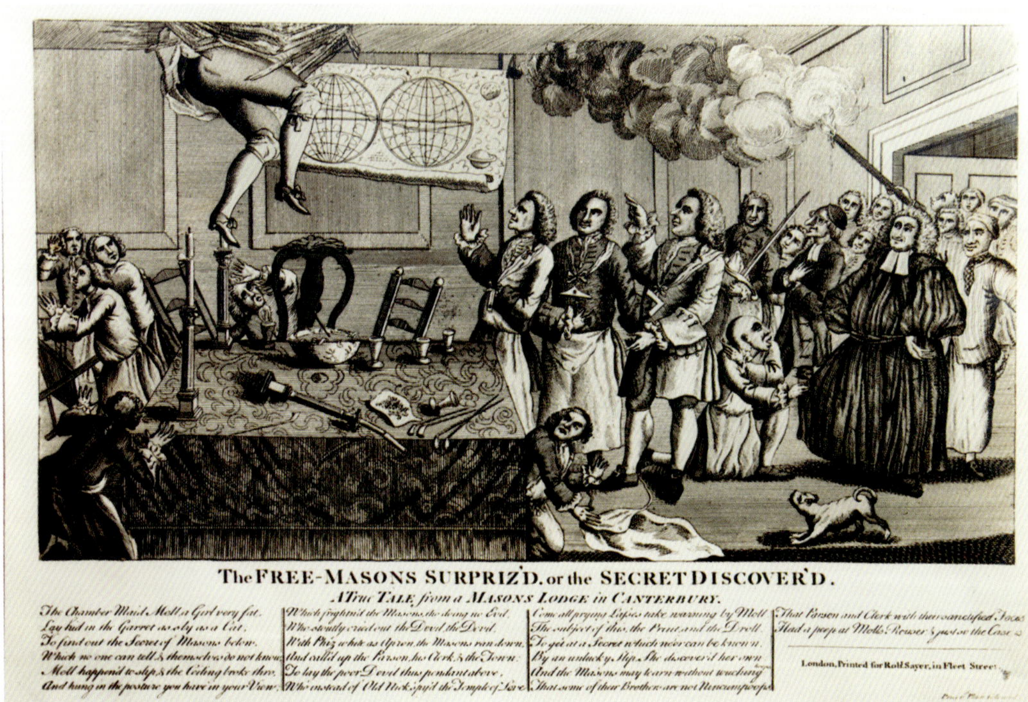

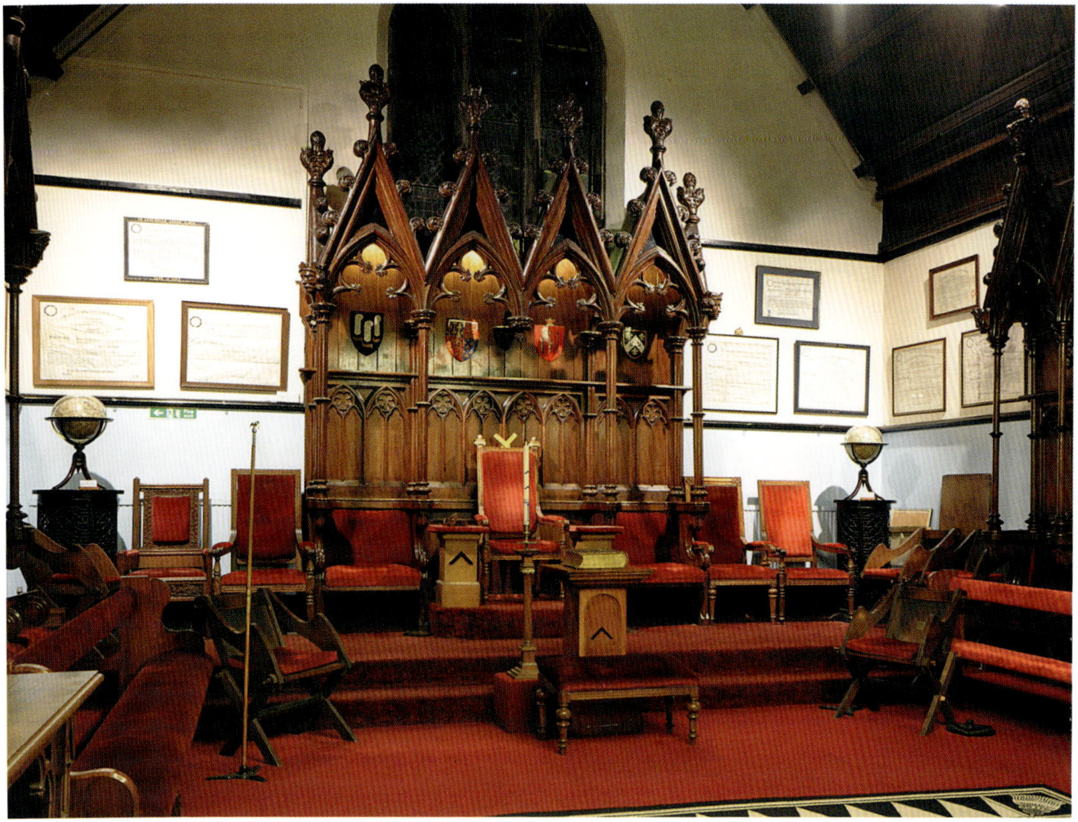

This photograph shows the interior of the **St Peter's Street temple** where ceremonies take place. The chair in the centre is where the Worshipful Master sits. You might like to compare this with the temple layout on page 12.

In 1880 the three lodges in Canterbury – United Industrious No.31, St Augustine No.972 and Royal Military No.1449 – which met in different hostelries, decided to have their own building where all lodges could meet. They purchased 38 St Peter's Street and the temple was built onto it in 1880. The museum adjoins it.

In the years since 1880 a number of other lodges, as well as other Orders, have been founded in Canterbury. Today twelve lodges, four chapters and ten other Orders use this temple for their meetings.

This edition © Scala Arts & Heritage Publishers Ltd, 2015
Text © The Kent Museum of Freemasonry, 2015

First published in 2015 by
Scala Arts & Heritage Publishers Ltd
10 Lion Yard
Tremadoc Road
London SW4 7NQ, UK
www.scalapublishers.com

In association with The Kent Museum of Freemasonry,
St Peter's Place, Canterbury, Kent CT1 2DA.

The writer would like to thank the Dean and Chapter of Canterbury Cathedral, Jeff Clarke of Falcon Display for permission to use photographs and graphics, and the Arthur Crick Trust for generous support of the project. Thanks also to John Howard, Tony Periton and Robin Evans for their unstinting help.

ISBN 978-1-85759-931-2

Written by Roger O'Brien
Photography and artwork by John Howard
Edited by Penny Worms
Designed by Nigel Soper
Printed in Turkey

10 9 8 7 6 5 4 3 2 1

All rights reserved. No part of this book may be reproduced, stored in a retrieval system or transmitted in any form or by any means electronic, mechanical, photocopying, recording or otherwise, without the written permission of The Kent Museum of Freemasonry and Scala Arts & Heritage Publishers Ltd.

Every effort has been made to acknowledge correct copyright of images where applicable. Any errors or omissions are unintentional and should be notified to the Publisher, who will arrange for corrections to appear in any reprints.

THE KENT MUSEUM
OF FREEMASONRY

FRONT COVER: Collar jewel showing the 'Invicta' prancing horse, the symbol of Kent.

BACK COVER: Apron of painted silk, showing King William III on horseback with various masonic symbols, dated 1688–90.

FRONT FLAP: A candle box, perhaps late eighteenth century, decorated with quill pens, suggesting the Lodge Secretary was in charge of it. He would have kept spare candles for the meetings in the days before electric light. The candles were kept under lock and key and probably given out sparingly.

BACK FLAP: The Kent Museum of Freemasonry, Canterbury.

INSIDE FRONT COVER: Glass goblet engraved with masonic symbols.

INSIDE BACK COVER: A print entitled 'Ceremony of Making a Free-Mason', c.1770.